Real World Colouring Book

For Advanced Users & Adults

50 Images

Created From Real Life Photos For You To Colour As You Please.

ISBN 978-0-359-82532-5

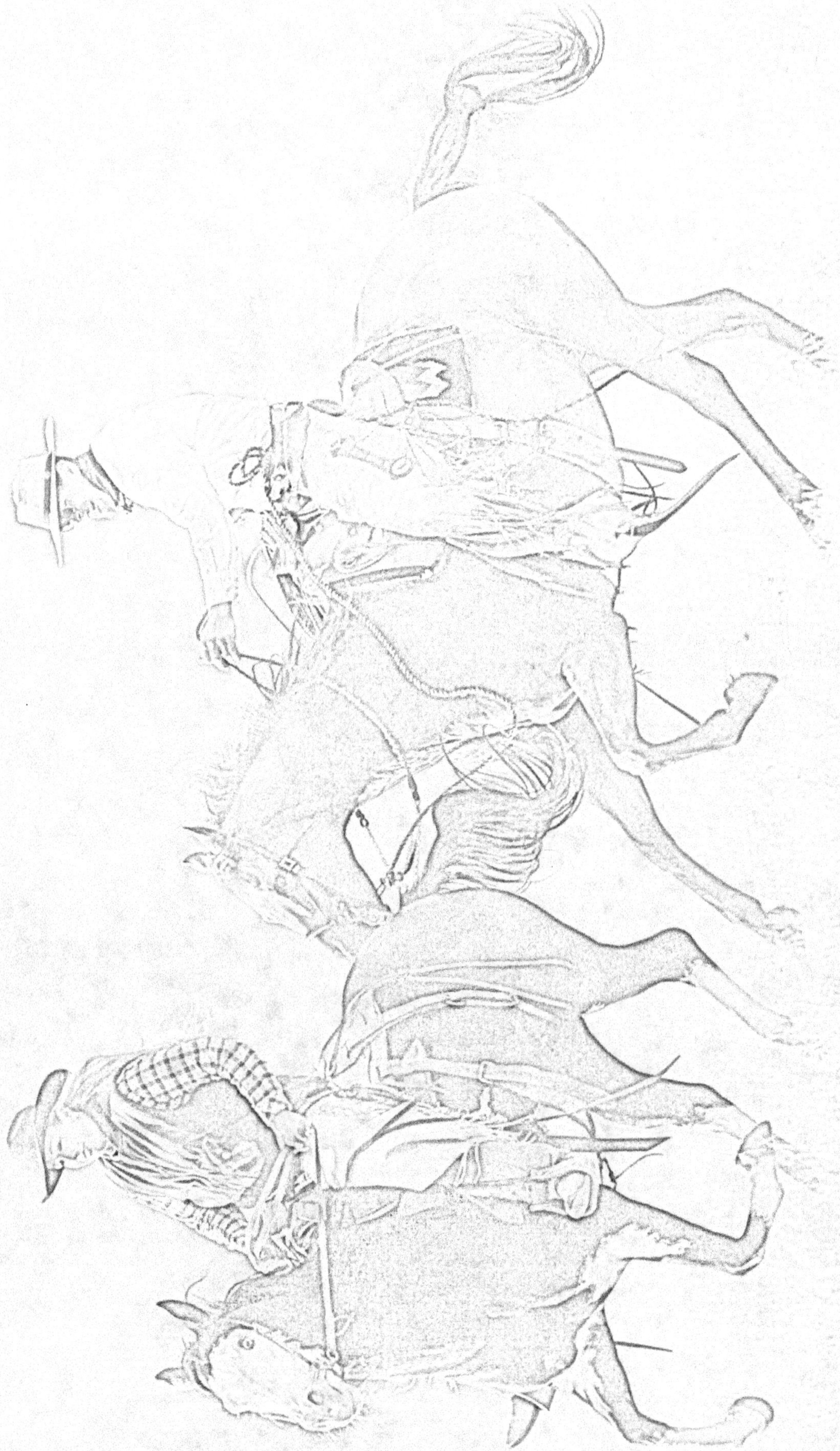

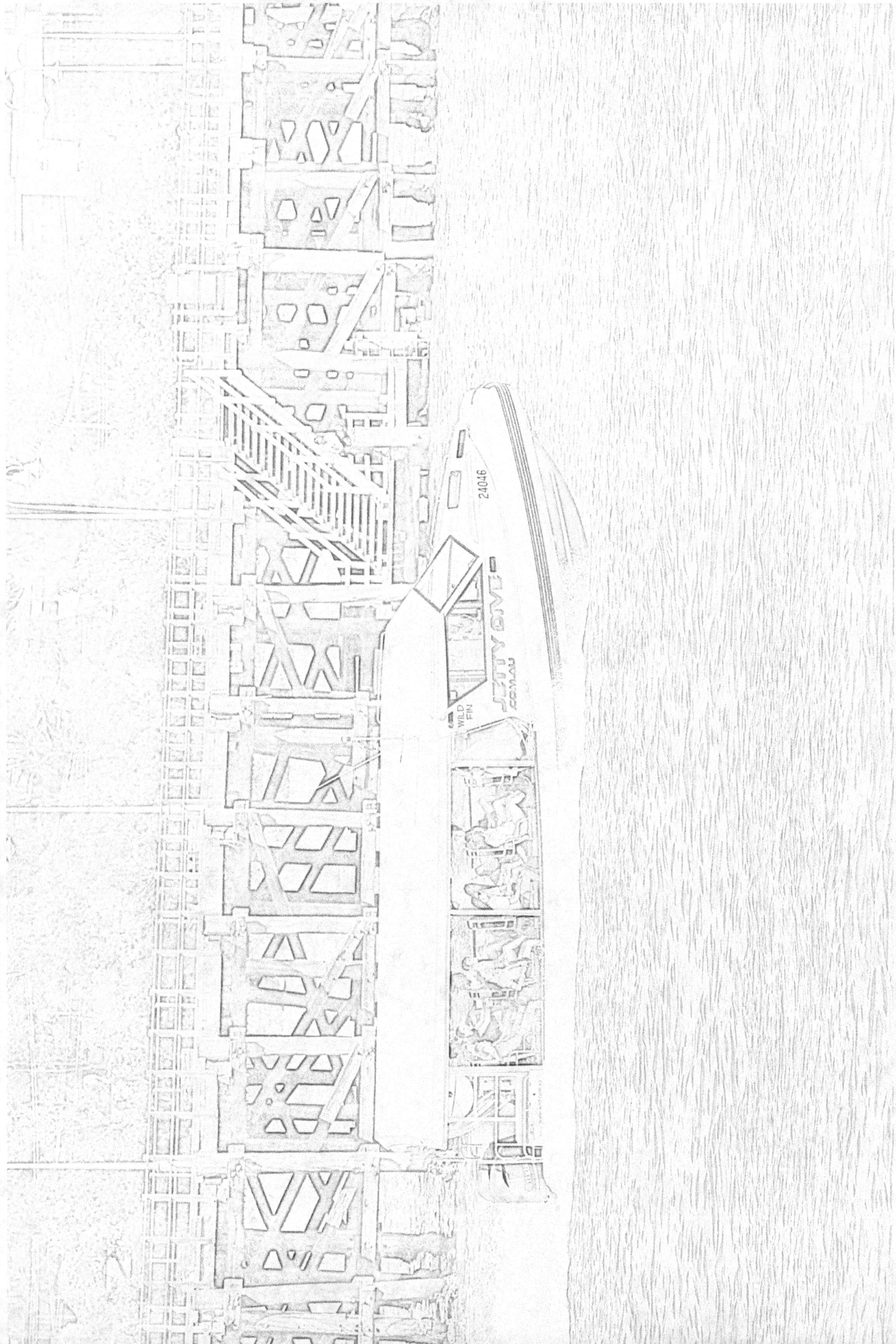
24046
WILD
FIN

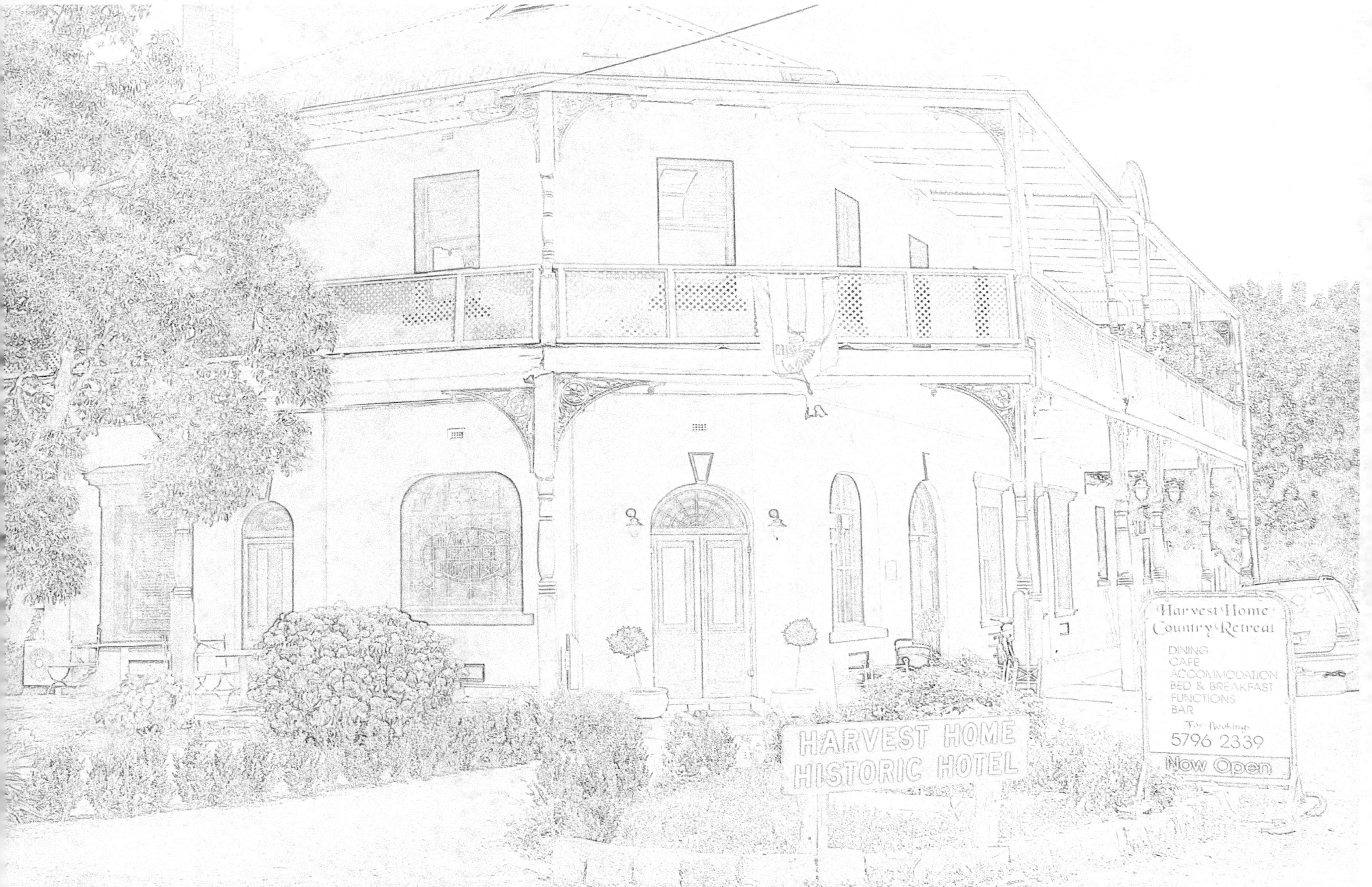

Harvest Home Country Retreat
DINING
CAFE
ACCOMMODATION
BED & BREAKFAST
FUNCTIONS
BAR
For Bookings
5796 2339
Now Open
HARVEST HOME
HISTORIC HOTEL

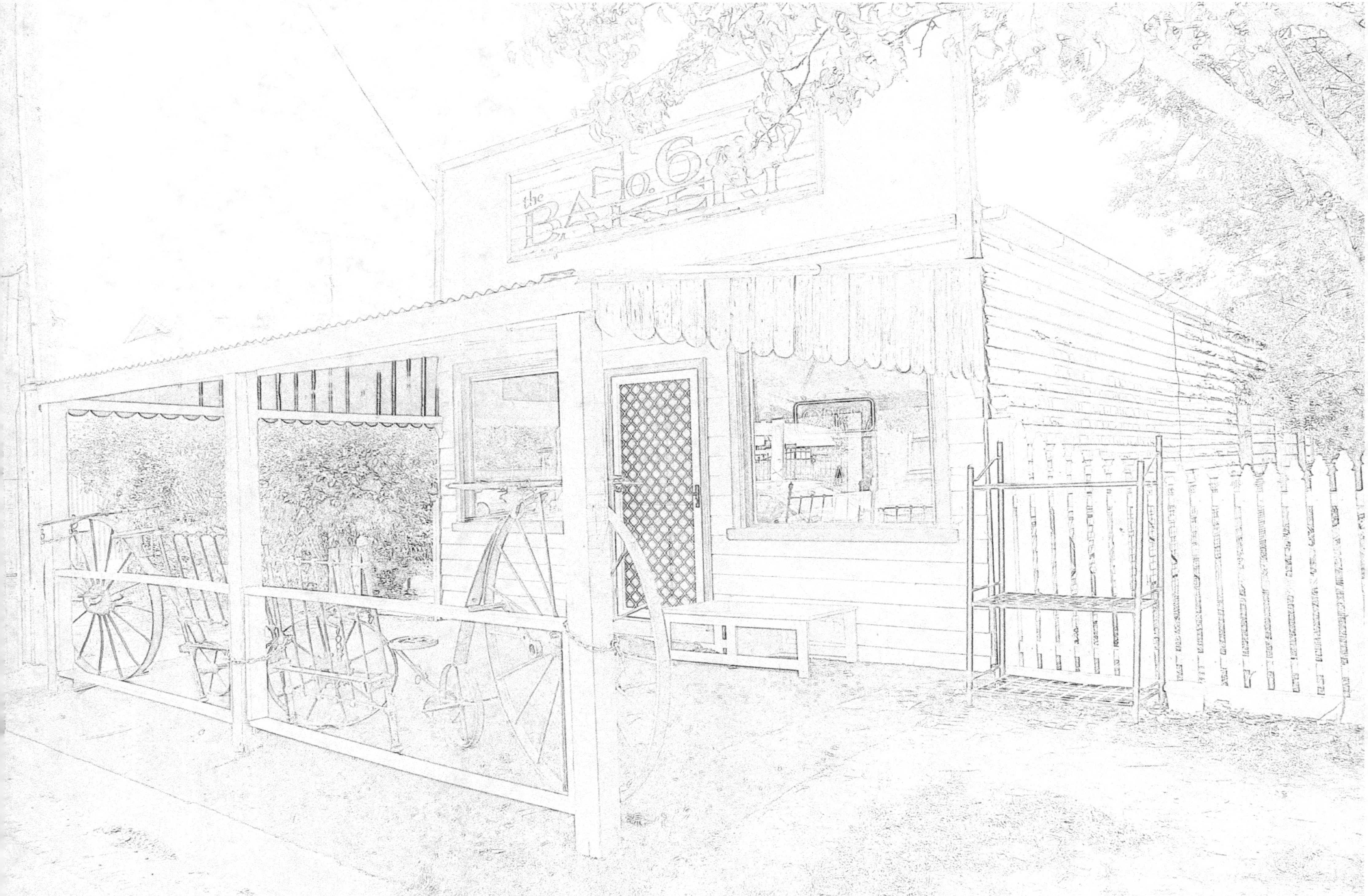
the
No. 6

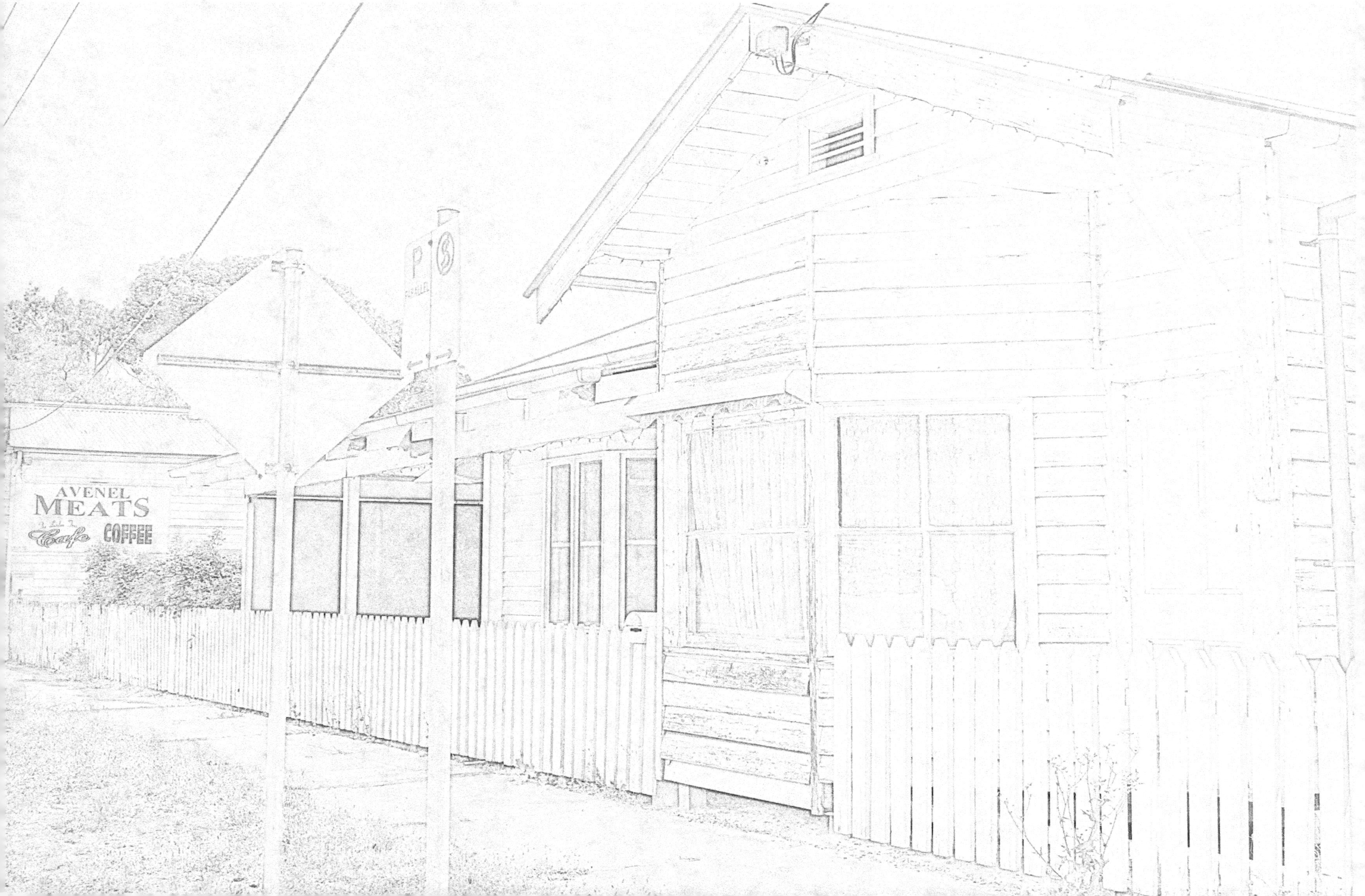
AVENEL
MEATS
Cafe
COFFEE
P

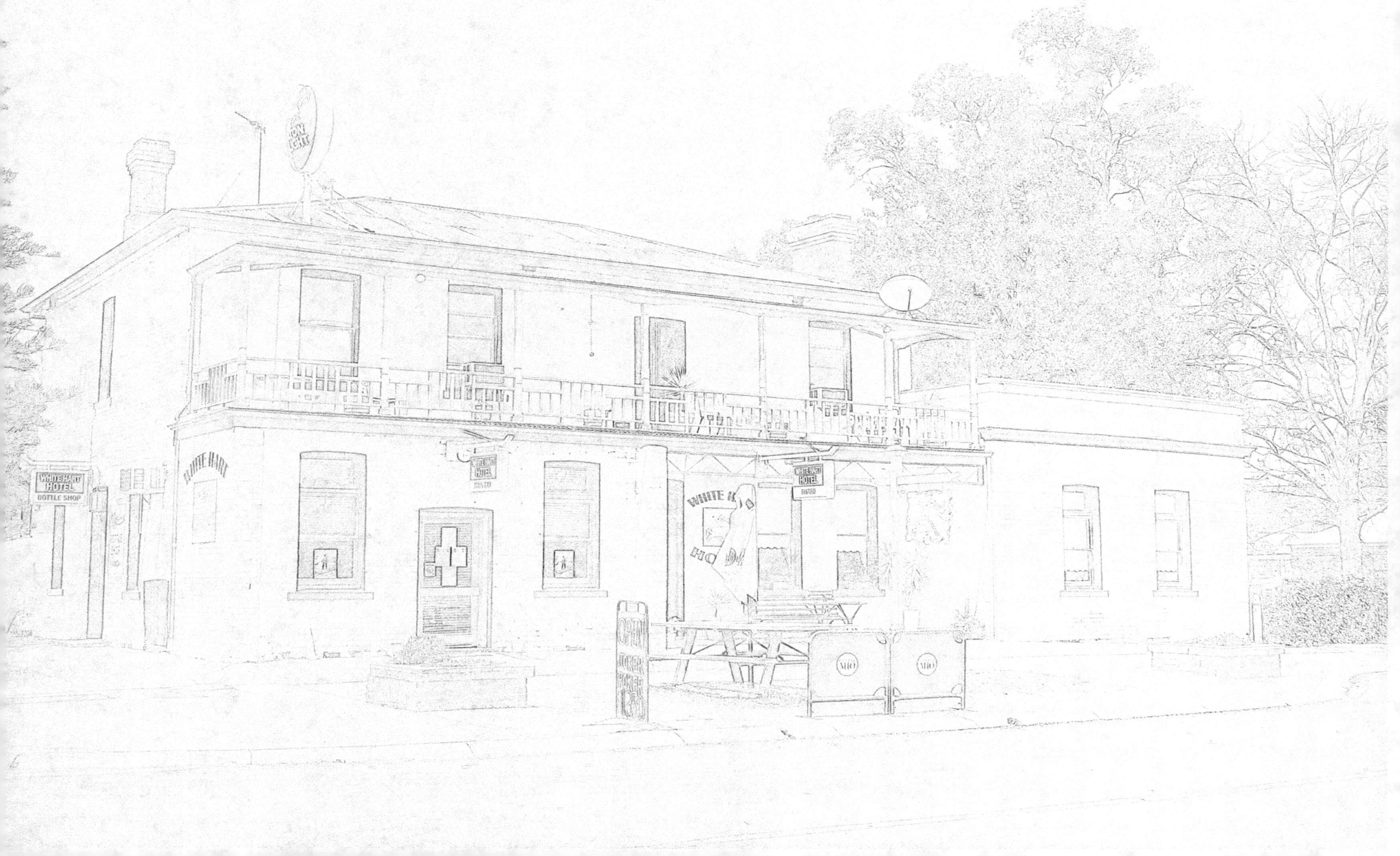
WHITE HART
HOTEL
BOTTLE SHOP
WHITE HART
HOTEL
BISTRO

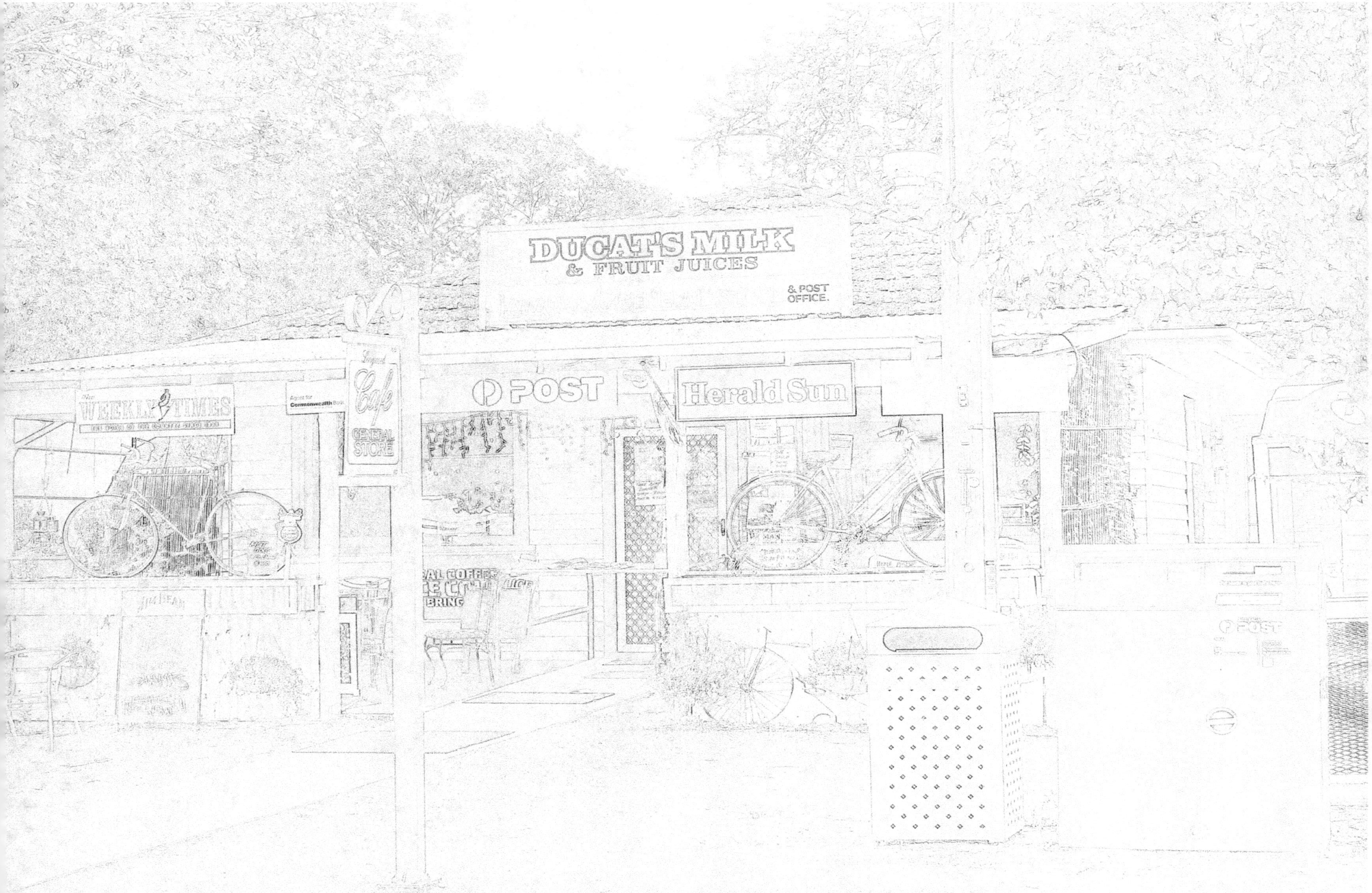
DUCAT'S MILK
& FRUIT JUICES
& POST OFFICE.
POST
Herald Sun
The WEEKLY TIMES
Cafe
GENERAL STORE
Agent for Commonwealth Bank
POST

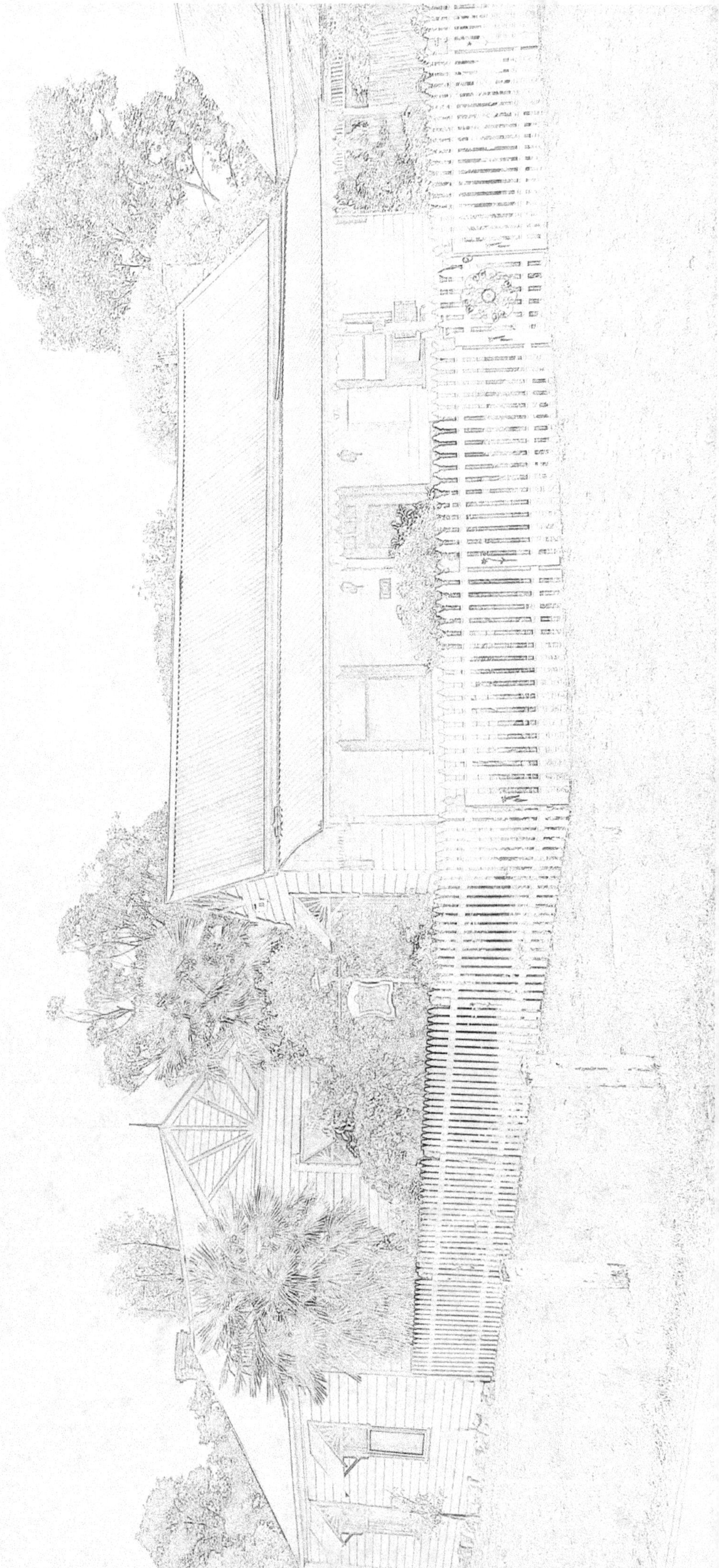

RAILWAY St

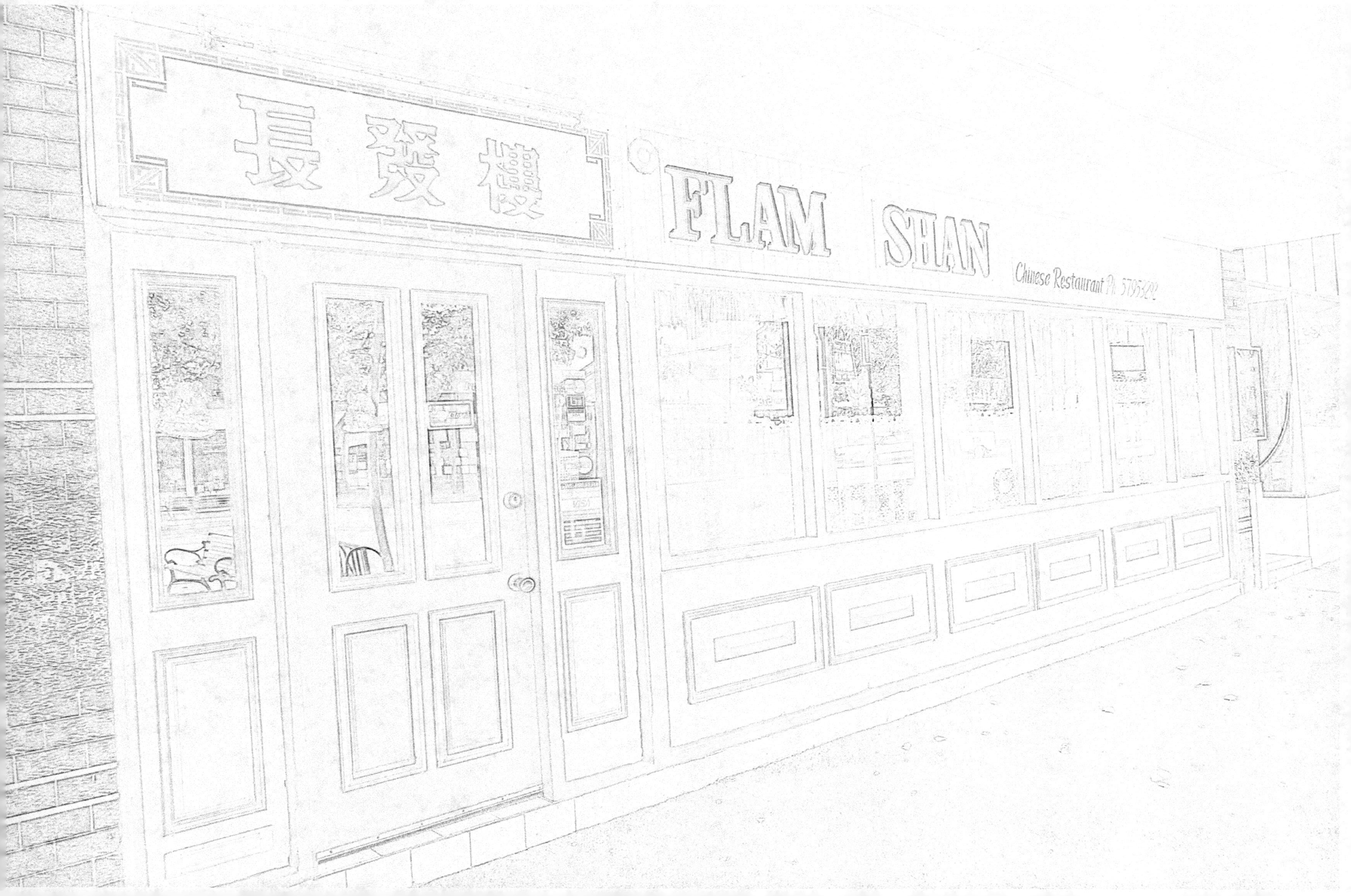
長發樓
FLAM SHAN
Chinese Restaurant Ph. 5795322

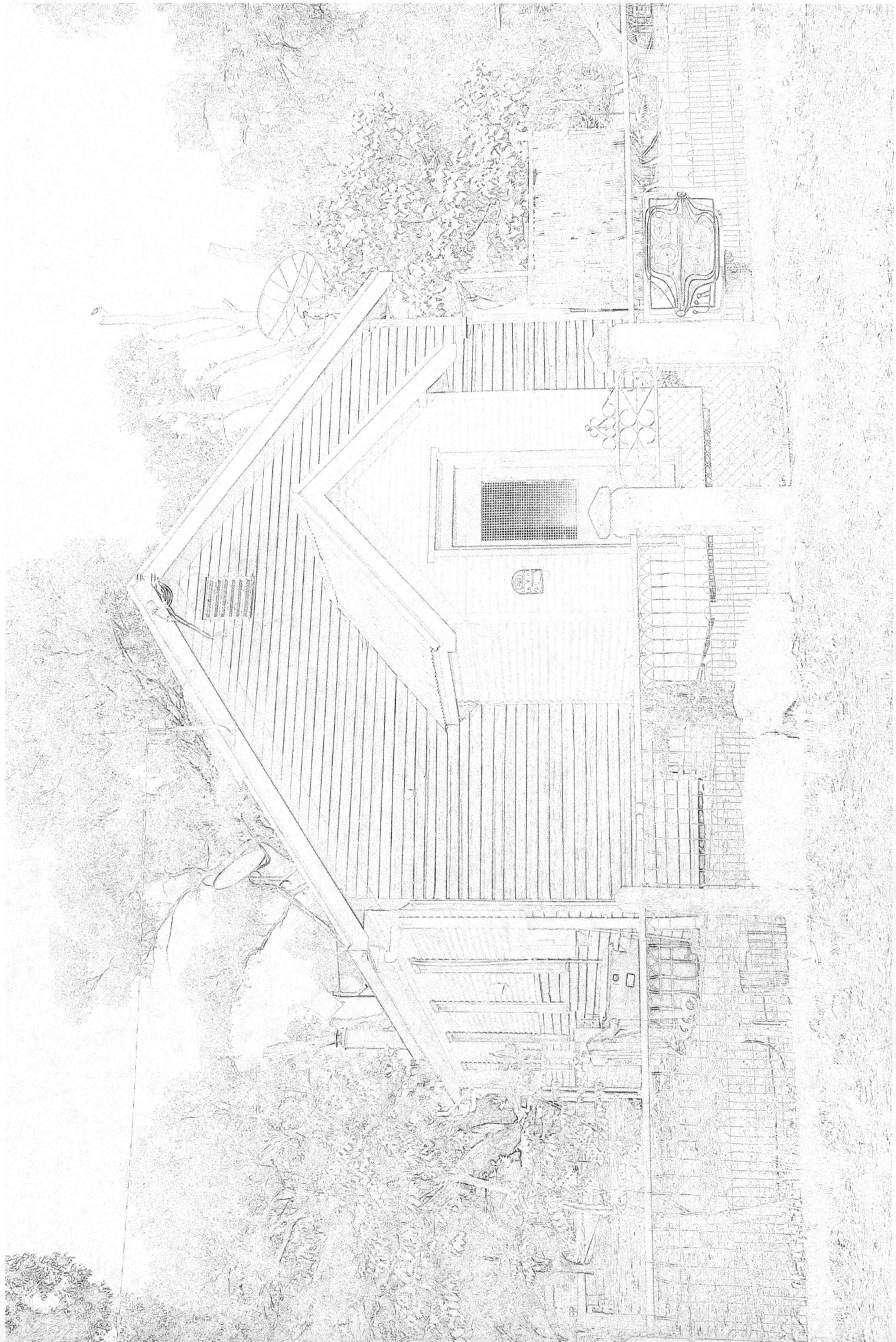

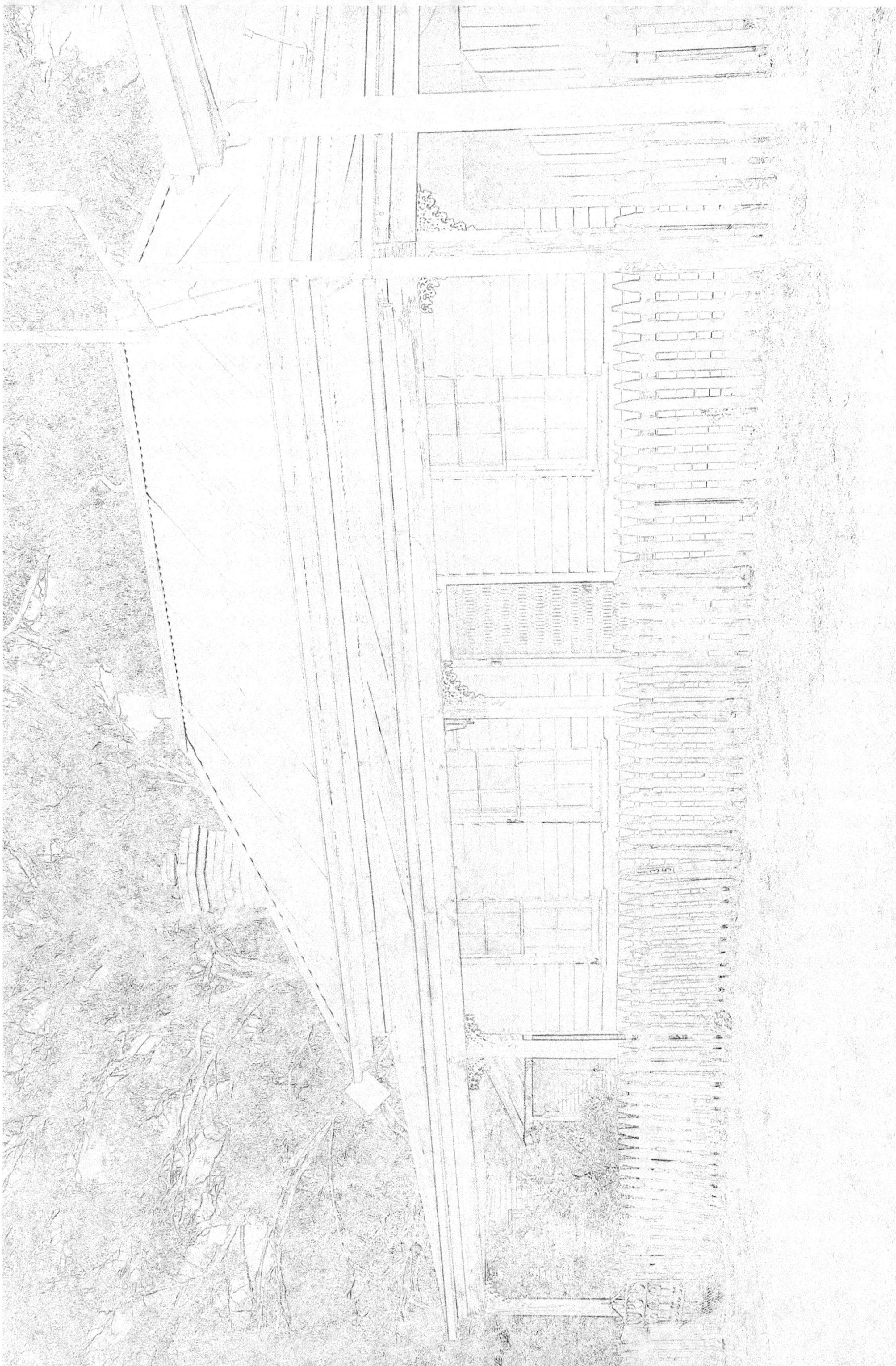

1905
MECHANICS INSTITUTE

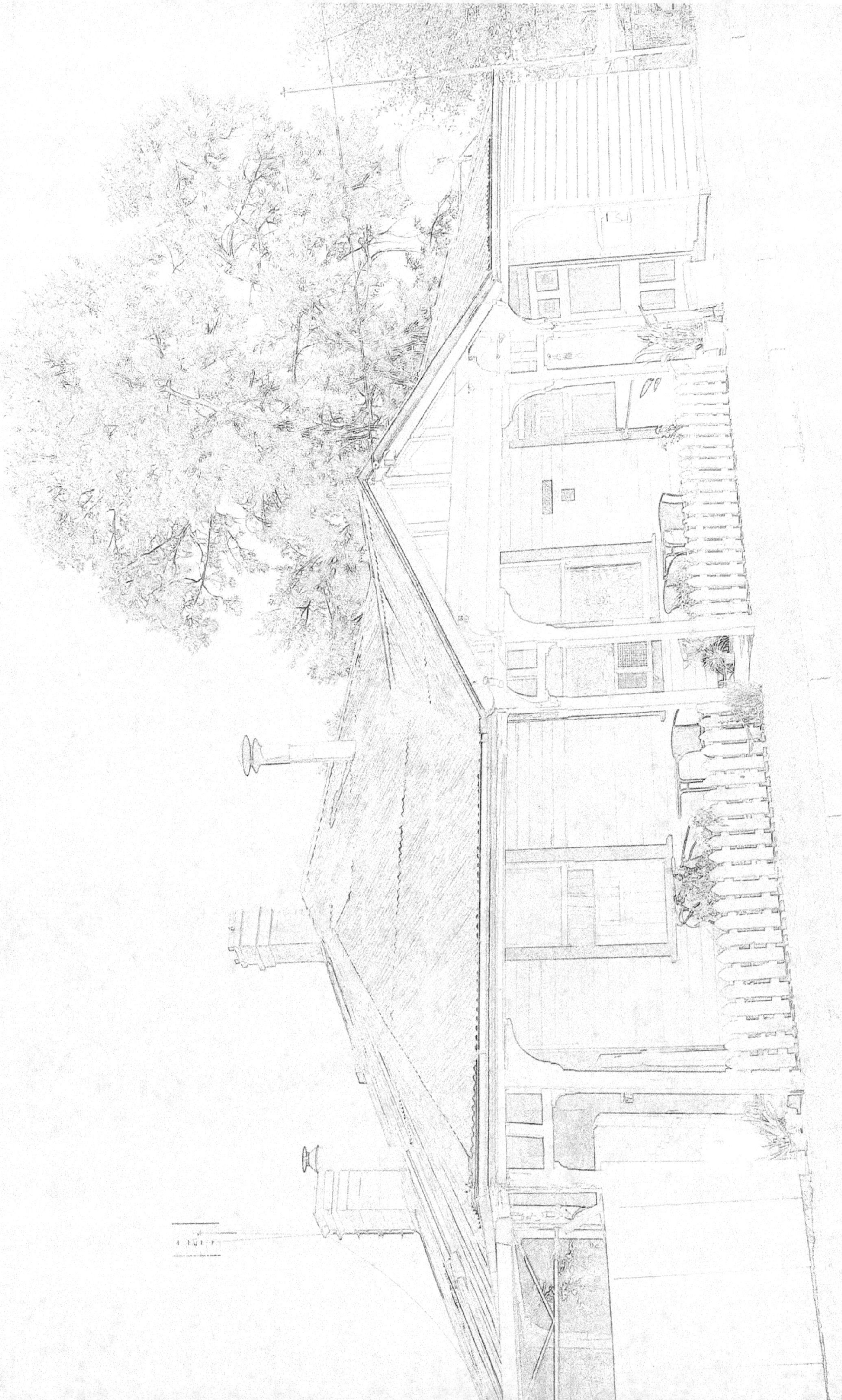

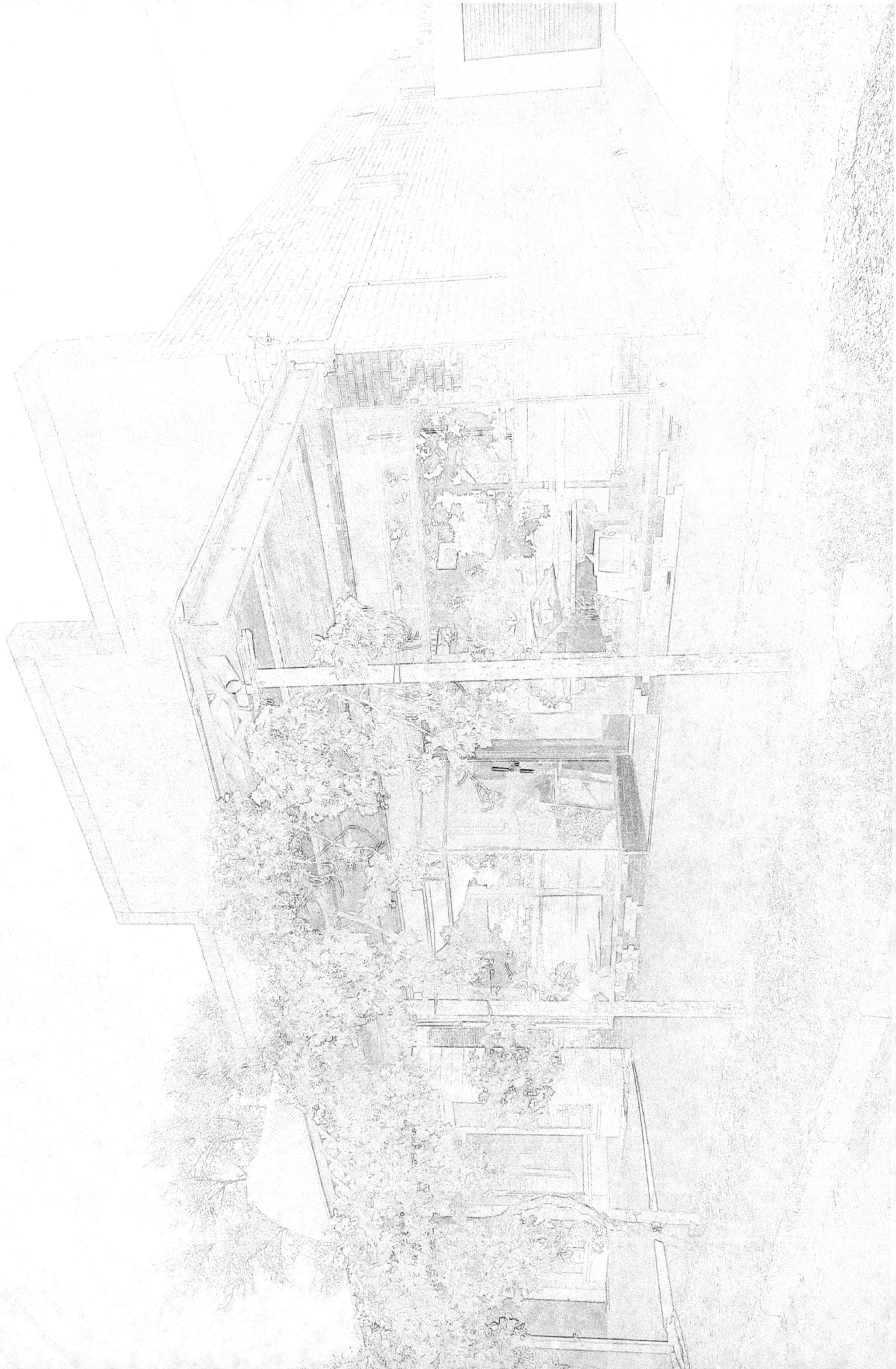

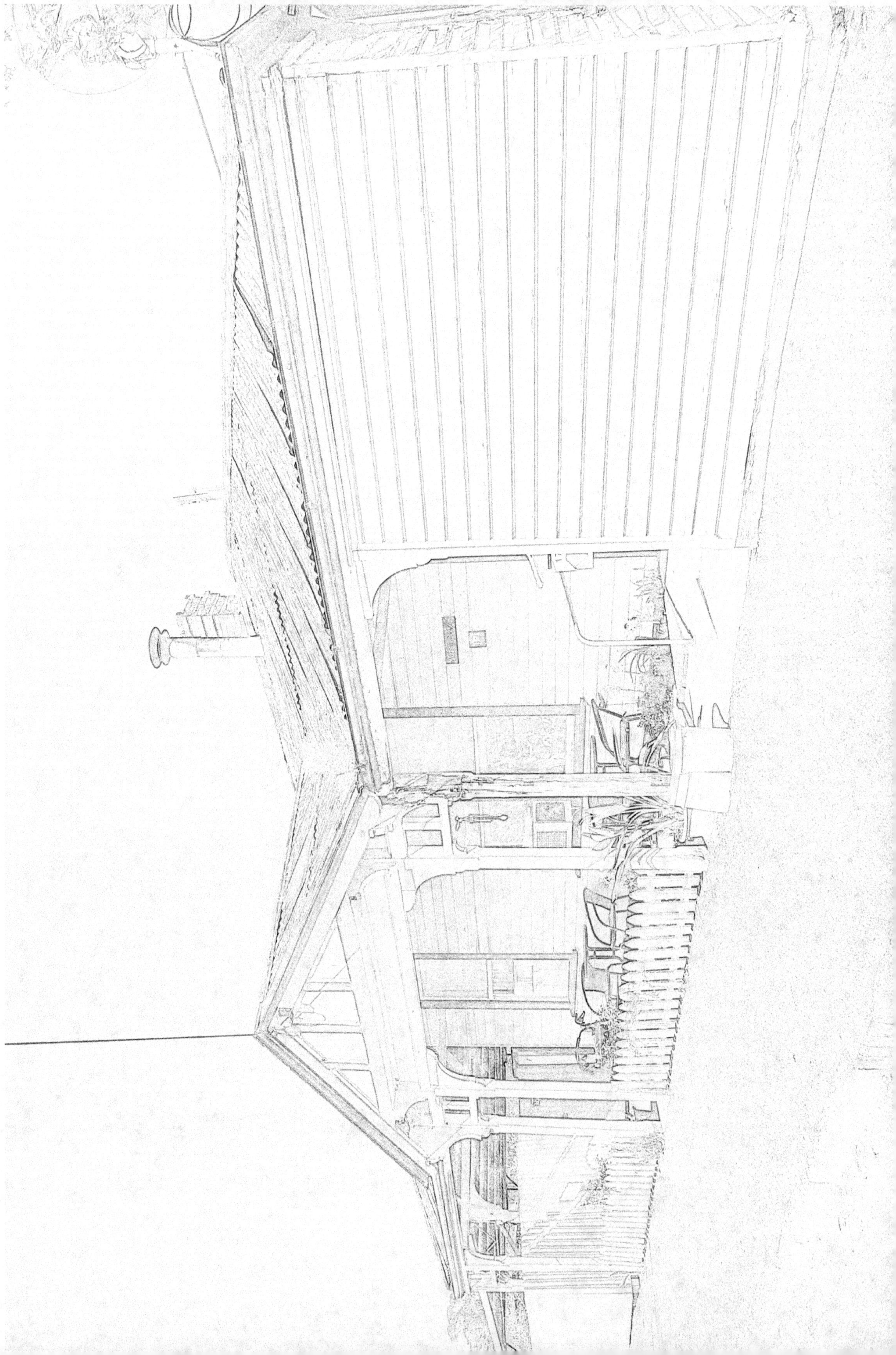

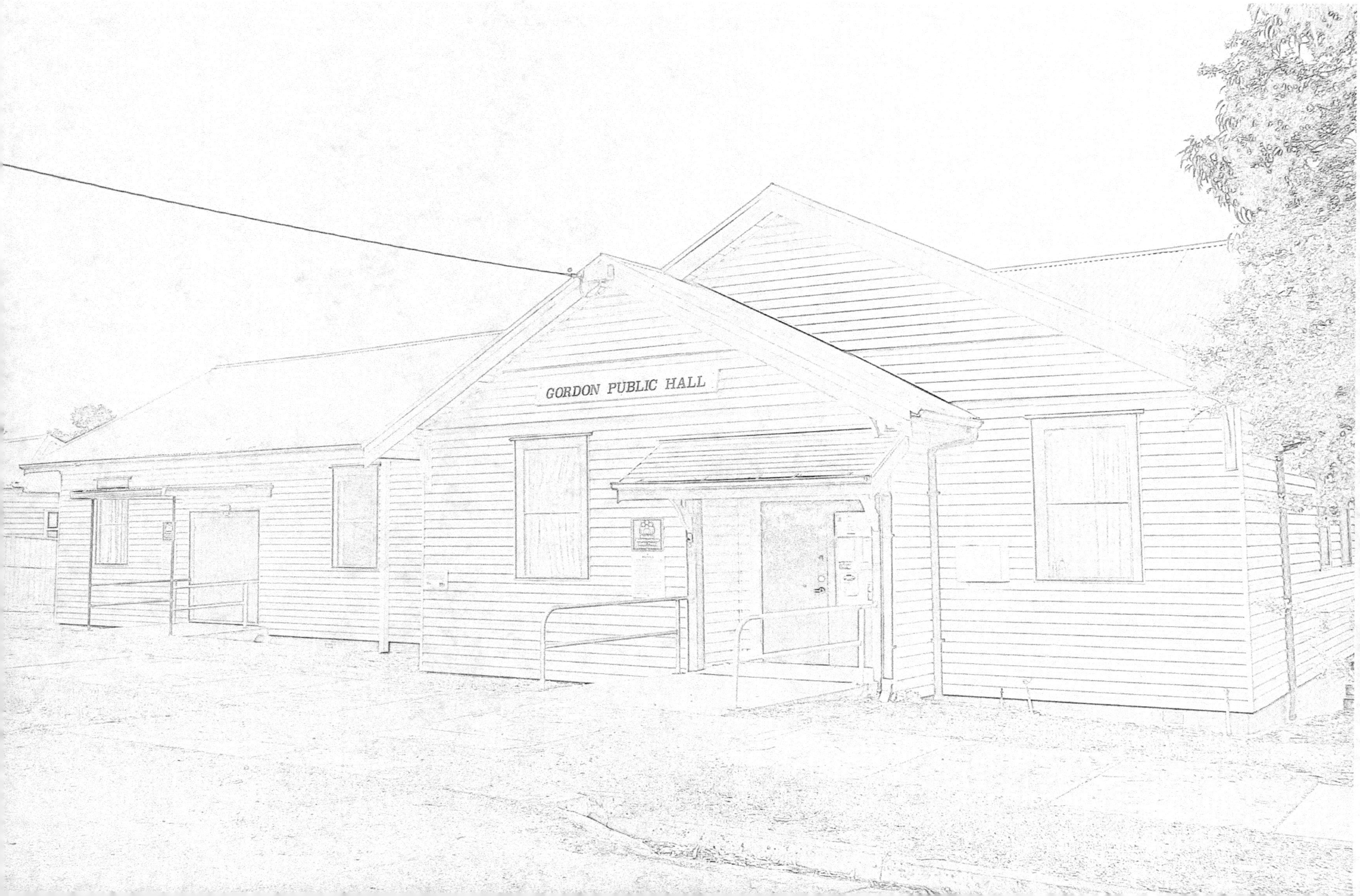
GORDON PUBLIC HALL

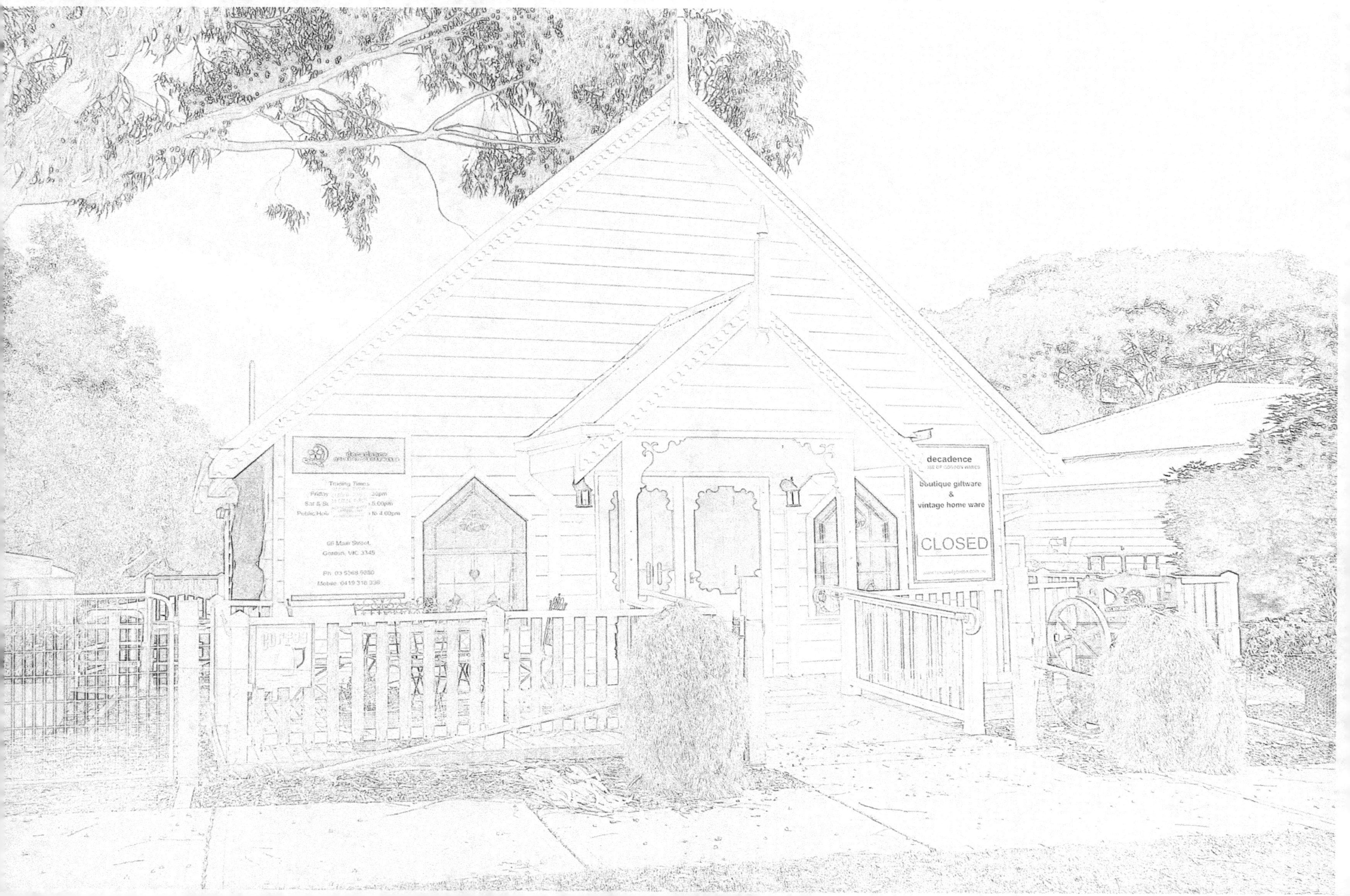
decadence
boutique giftware
&
vintage home ware
CLOSED
Trading Times
68 Main Street,
Gordon, VIC 3345

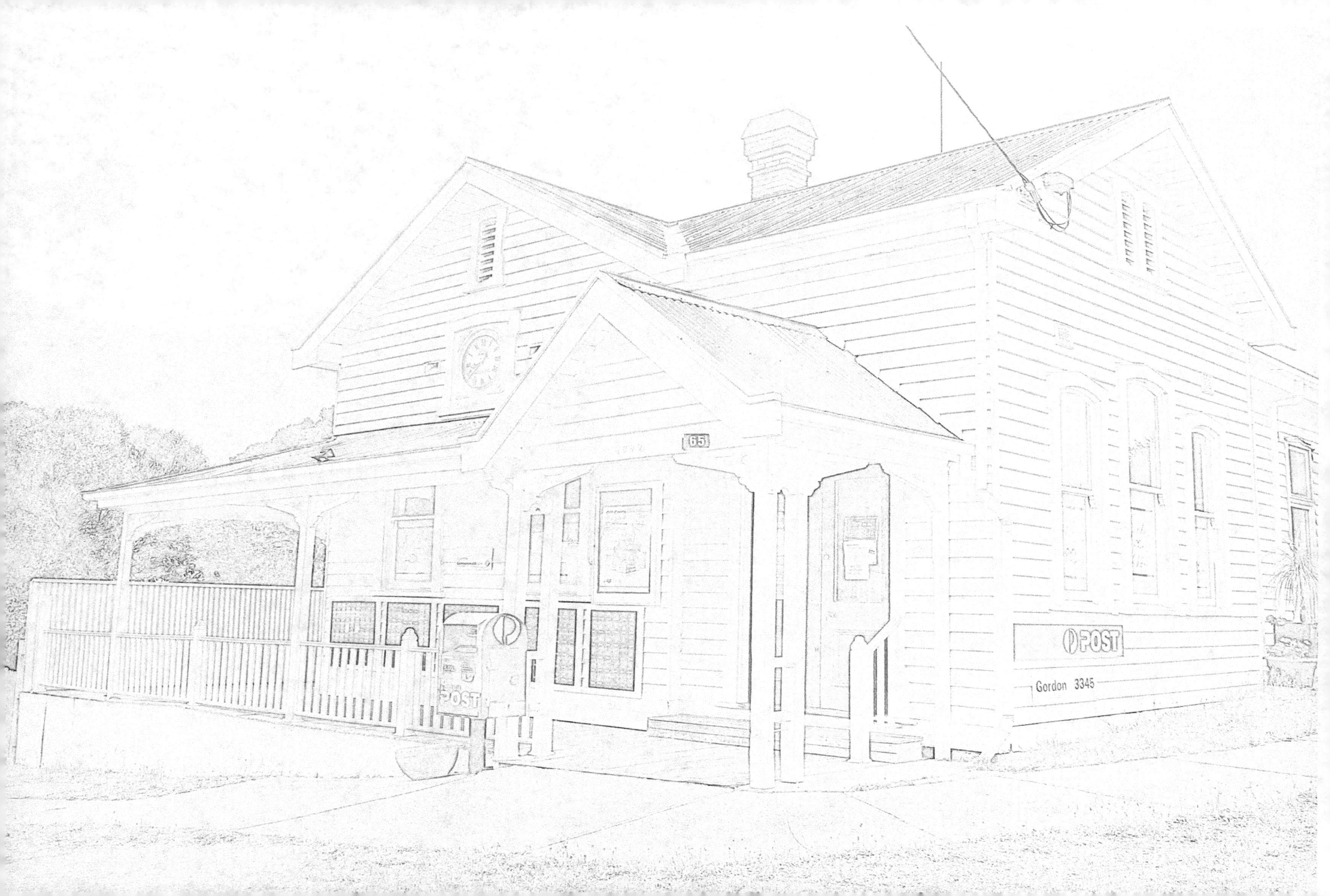
65
POST
Gordon 3345
POST

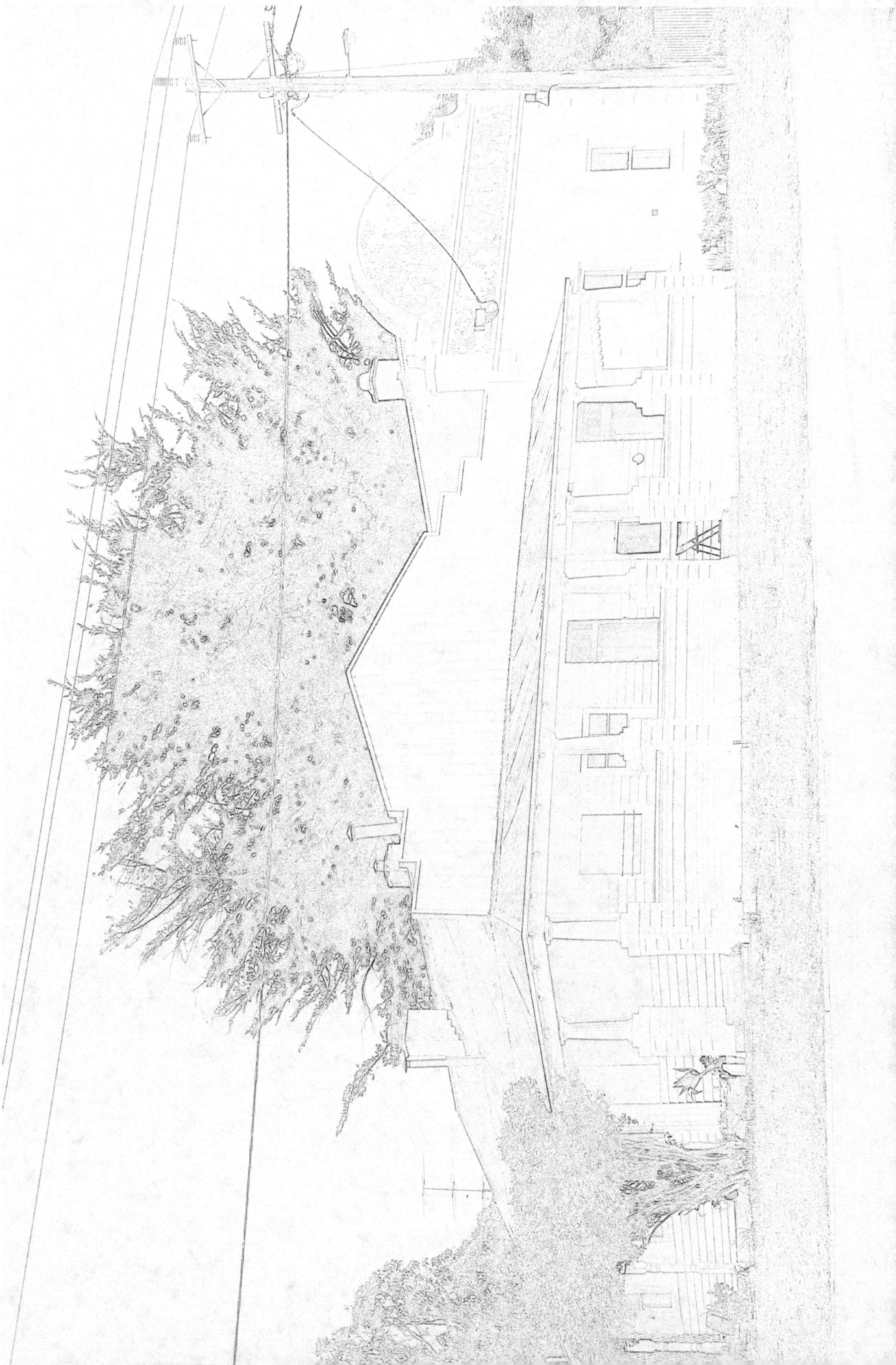

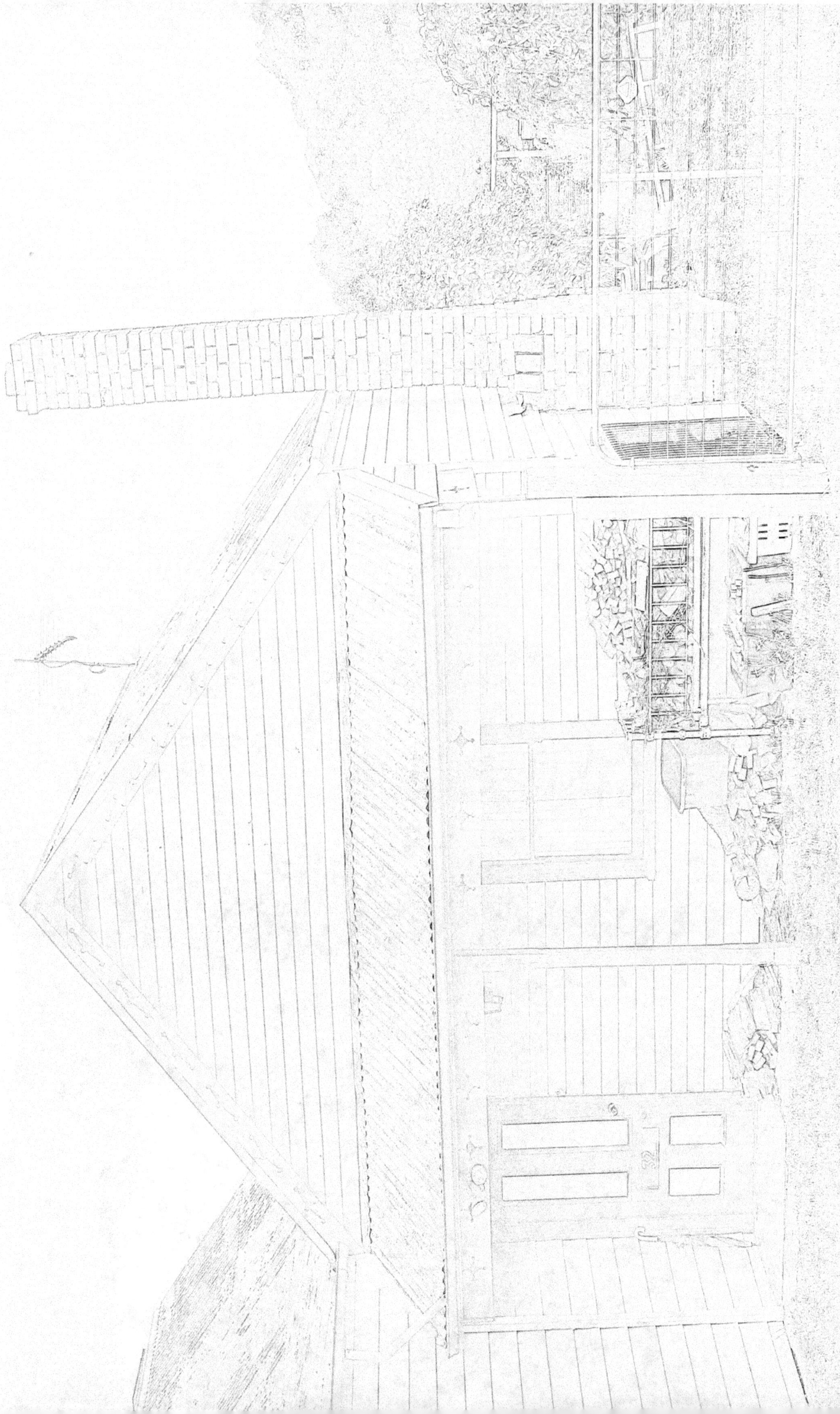

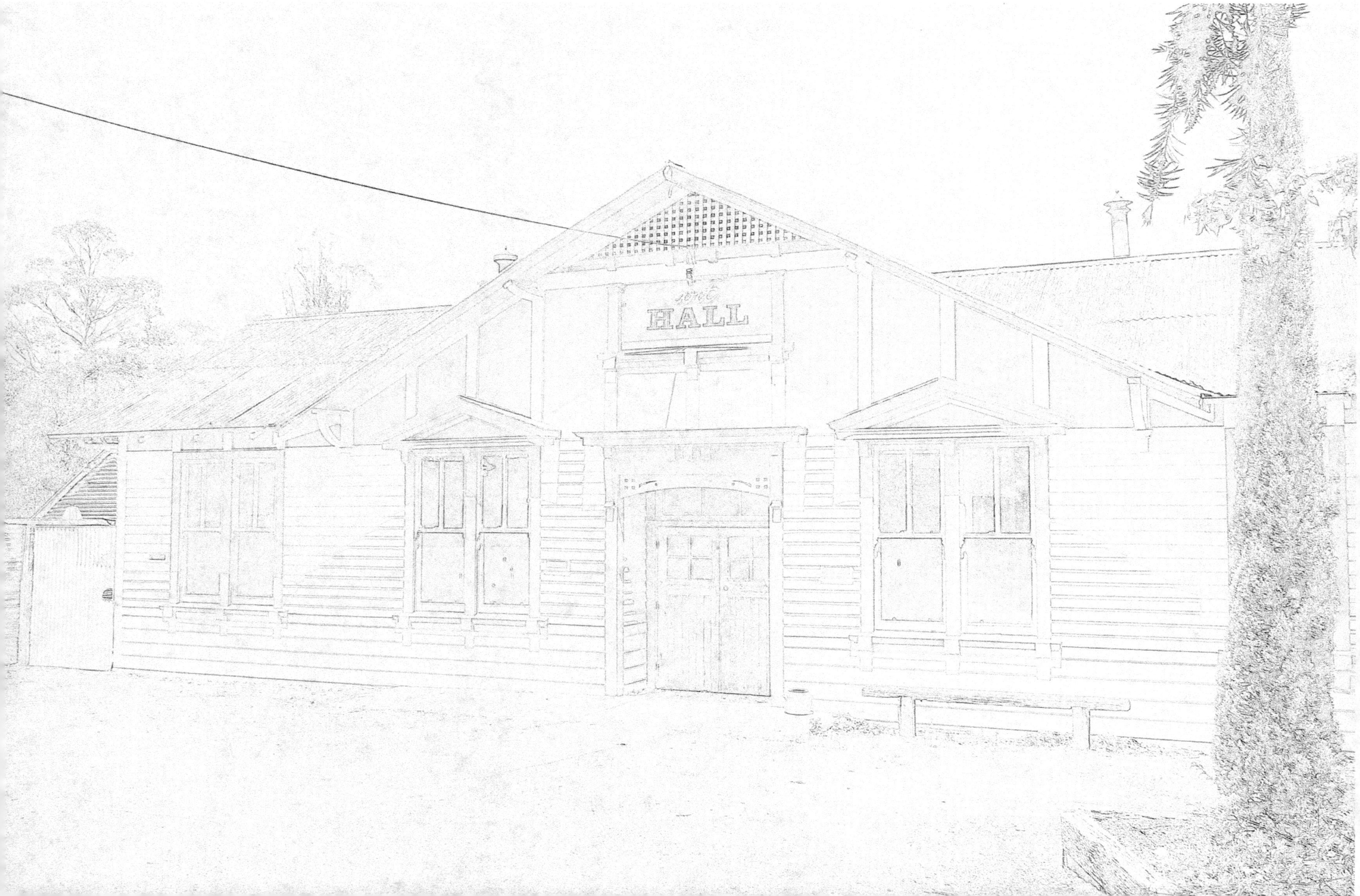
HALL

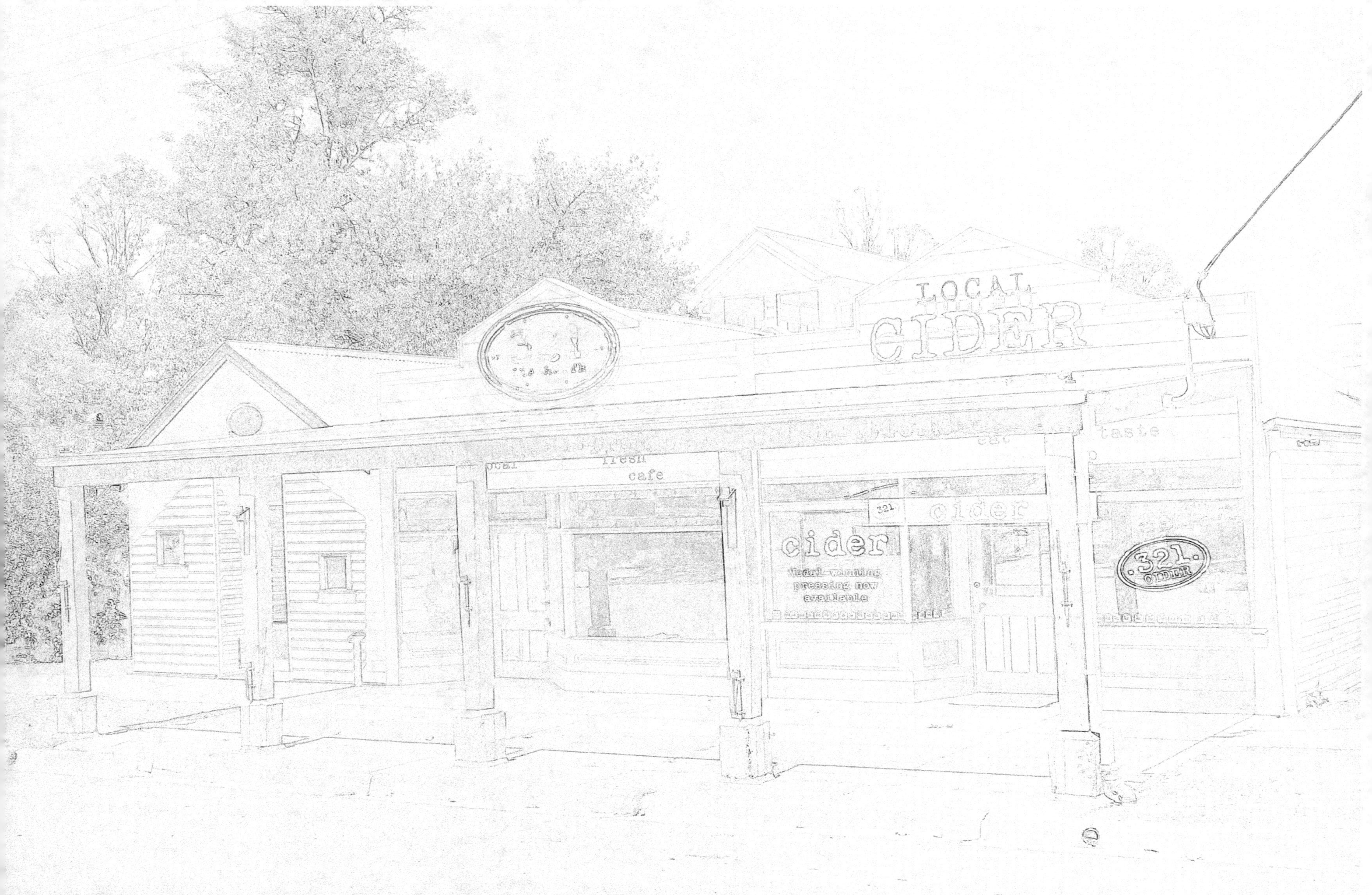
LOCAL
CIDER
cafe
taste
321
cider
cider
pressing now
available
.321.
CIDER

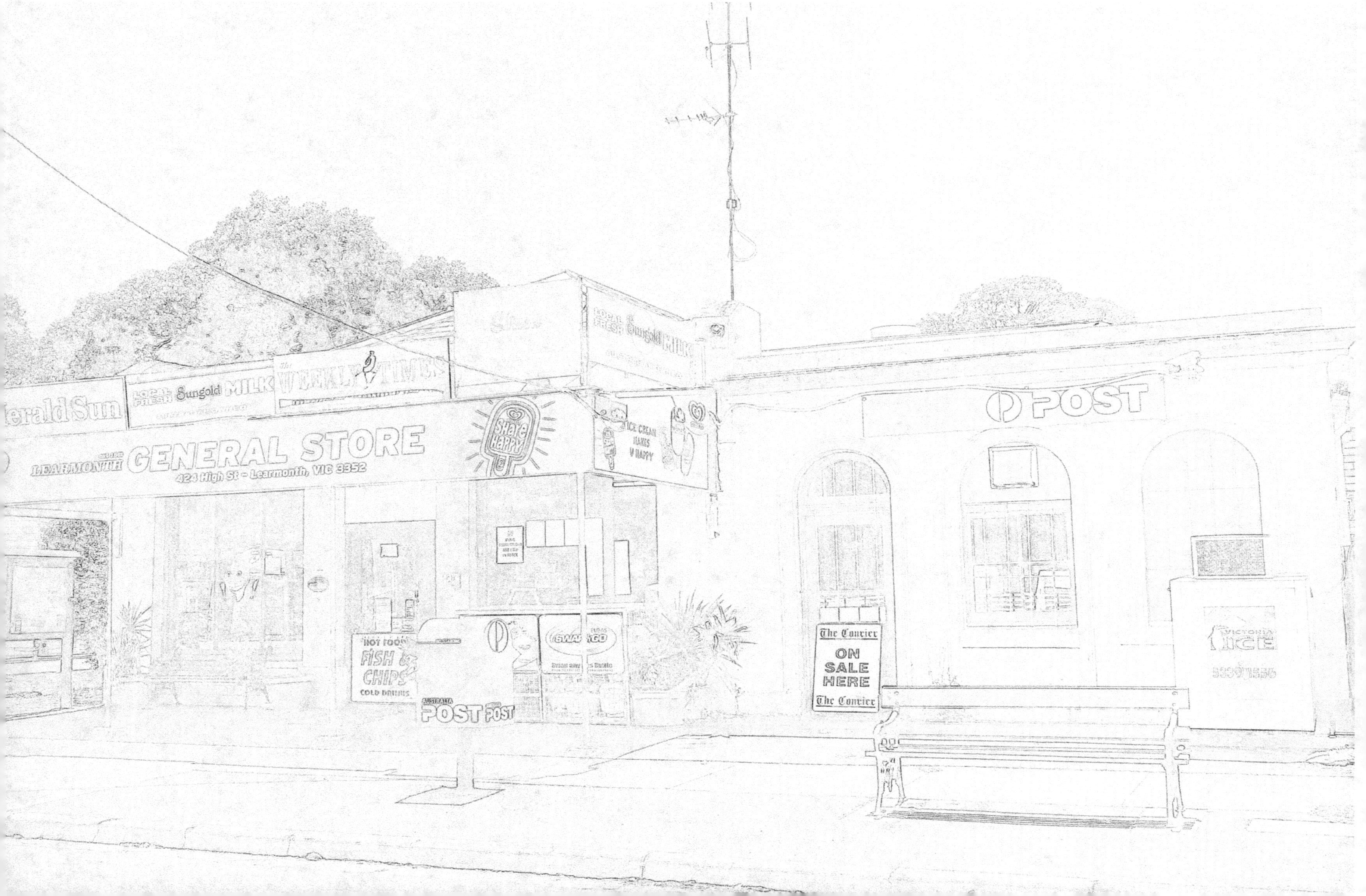

erald Sun
LOCAL FRESH Sungold MILK
The WEEKLY TIMES
LEARMONTH GENERAL STORE
424 High St - Learmonth, VIC 3352
Share Happy
ICE CREAM MAKES U HAPPY
POST
The Courier
ON SALE HERE
The Courier
HOT FOOD
FISH & CHIPS
COLD DRINKS
AUSTRALIA POST
POST
VICTORIA ICE

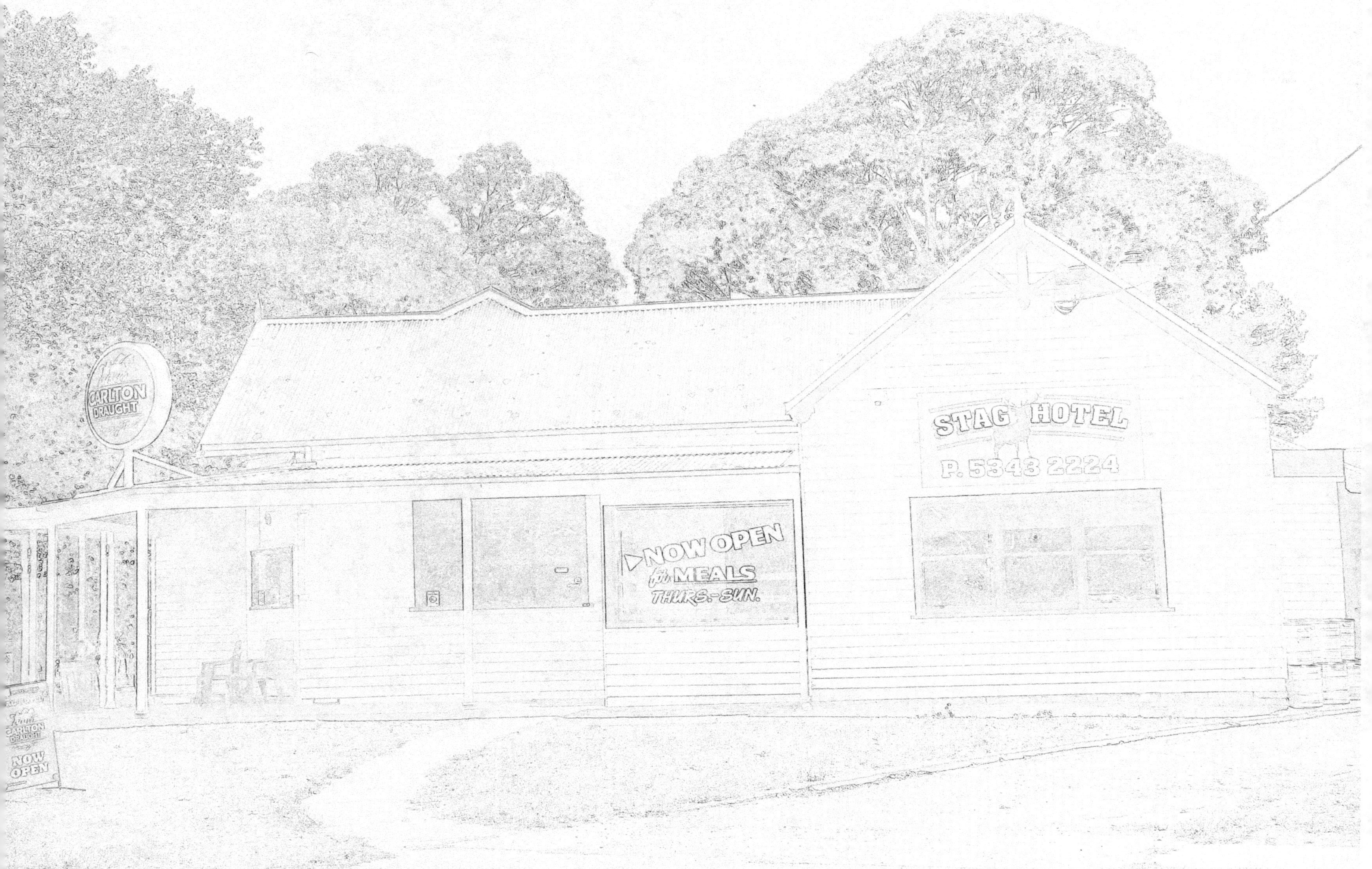
CARLTON DRAUGHT
STAG HOTEL
P. 5343 2224
NOW OPEN
MEALS
THURS.-SUN.
CARLTON DRAUGHT
NOW OPEN

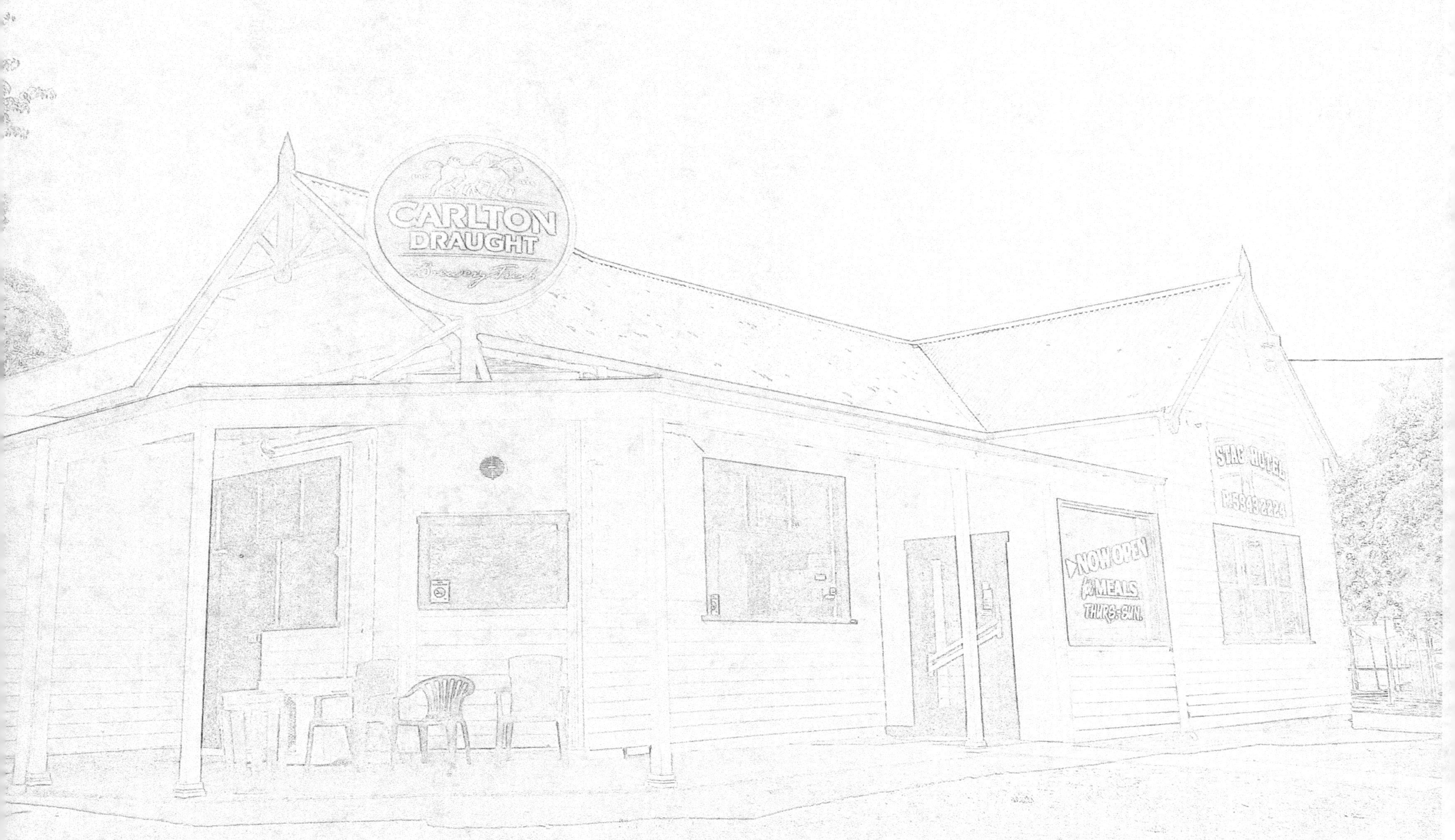
CARLTON
DRAUGHT
STAG HOTEL
5943 2224
NOW OPEN
MEALS
THURS-SUN.

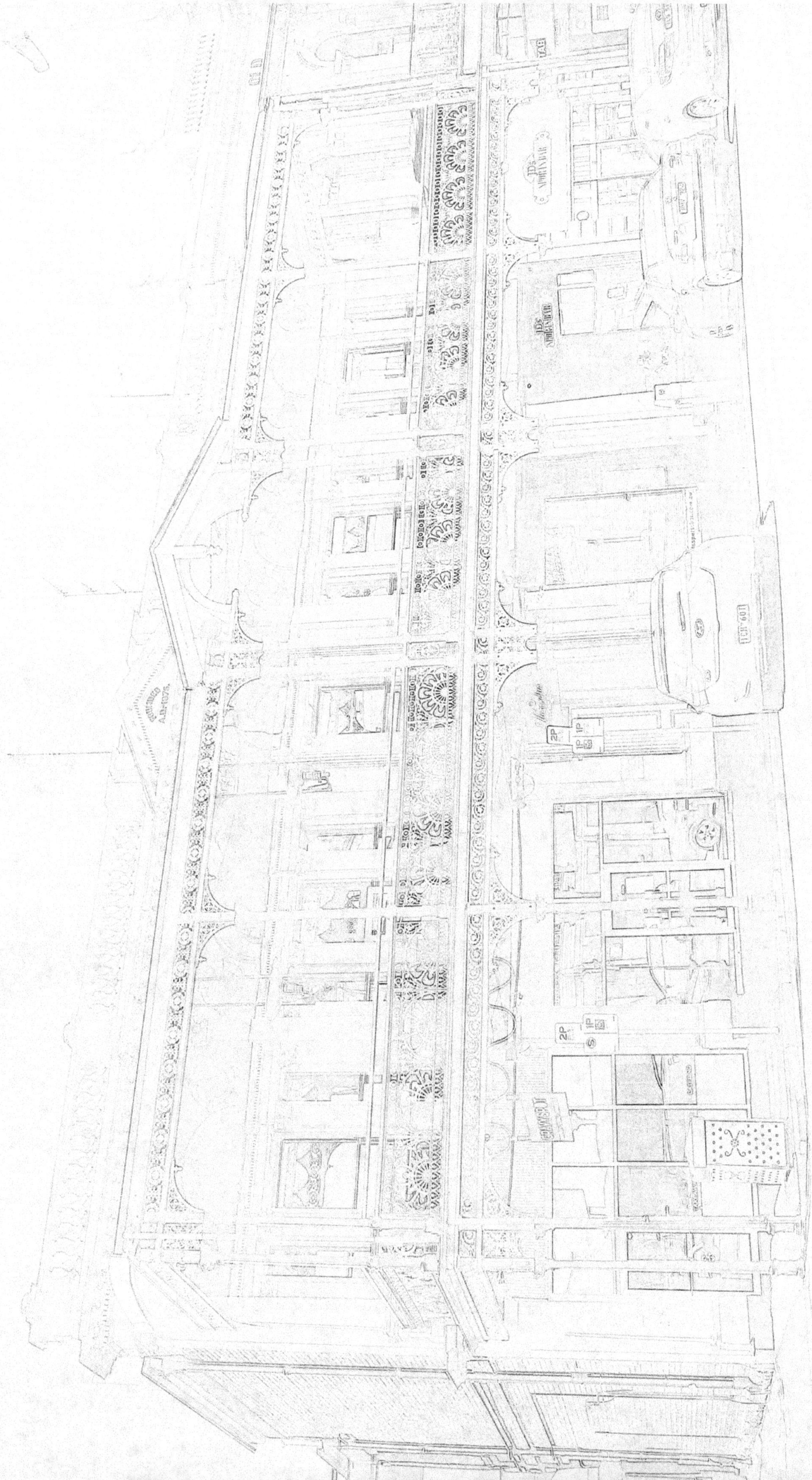

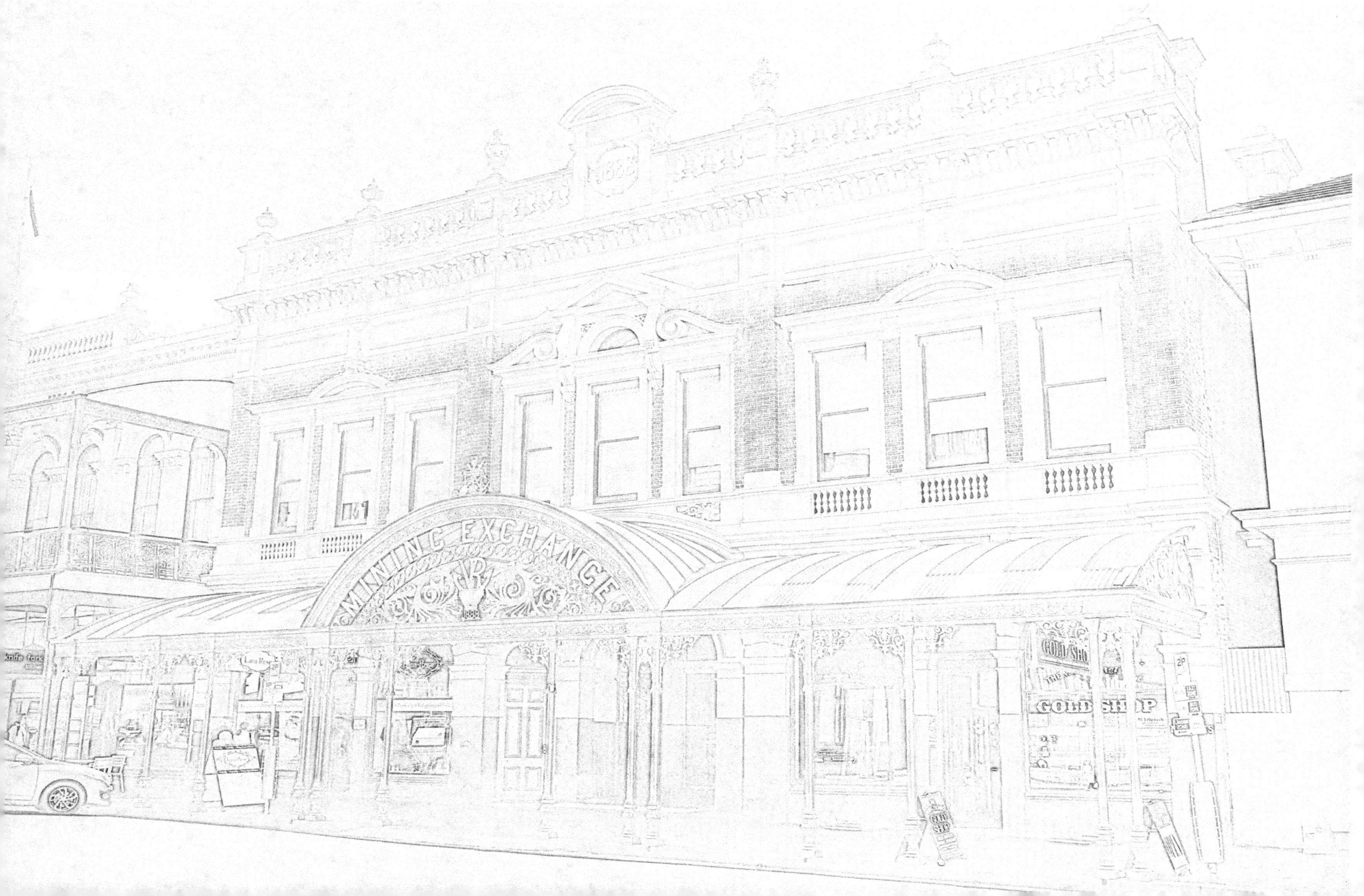
MINING EXCHANGE
1888
GOLD SHOP

Proudly supporting the Ballarat CommUnity
Bendigo Bank
14

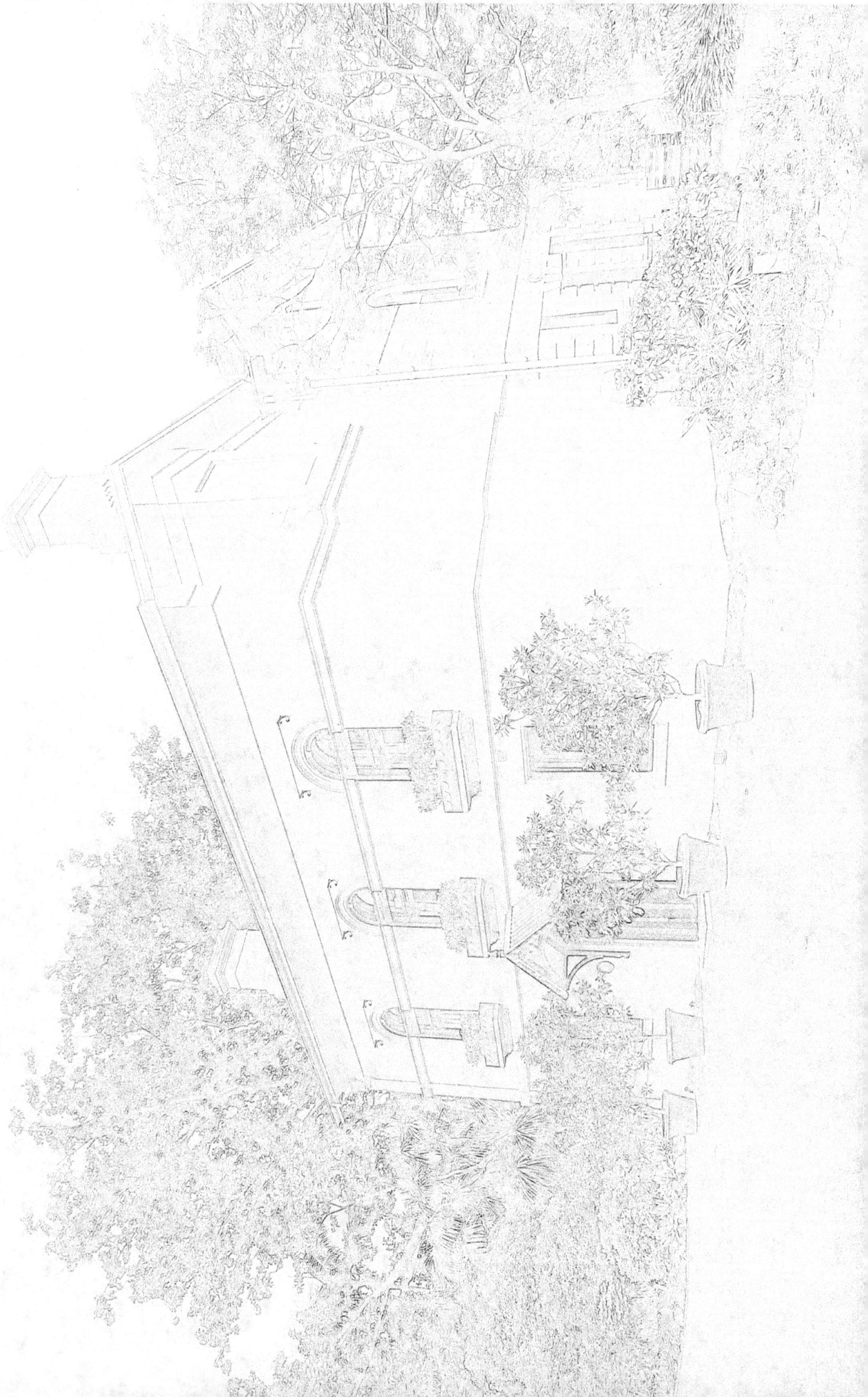

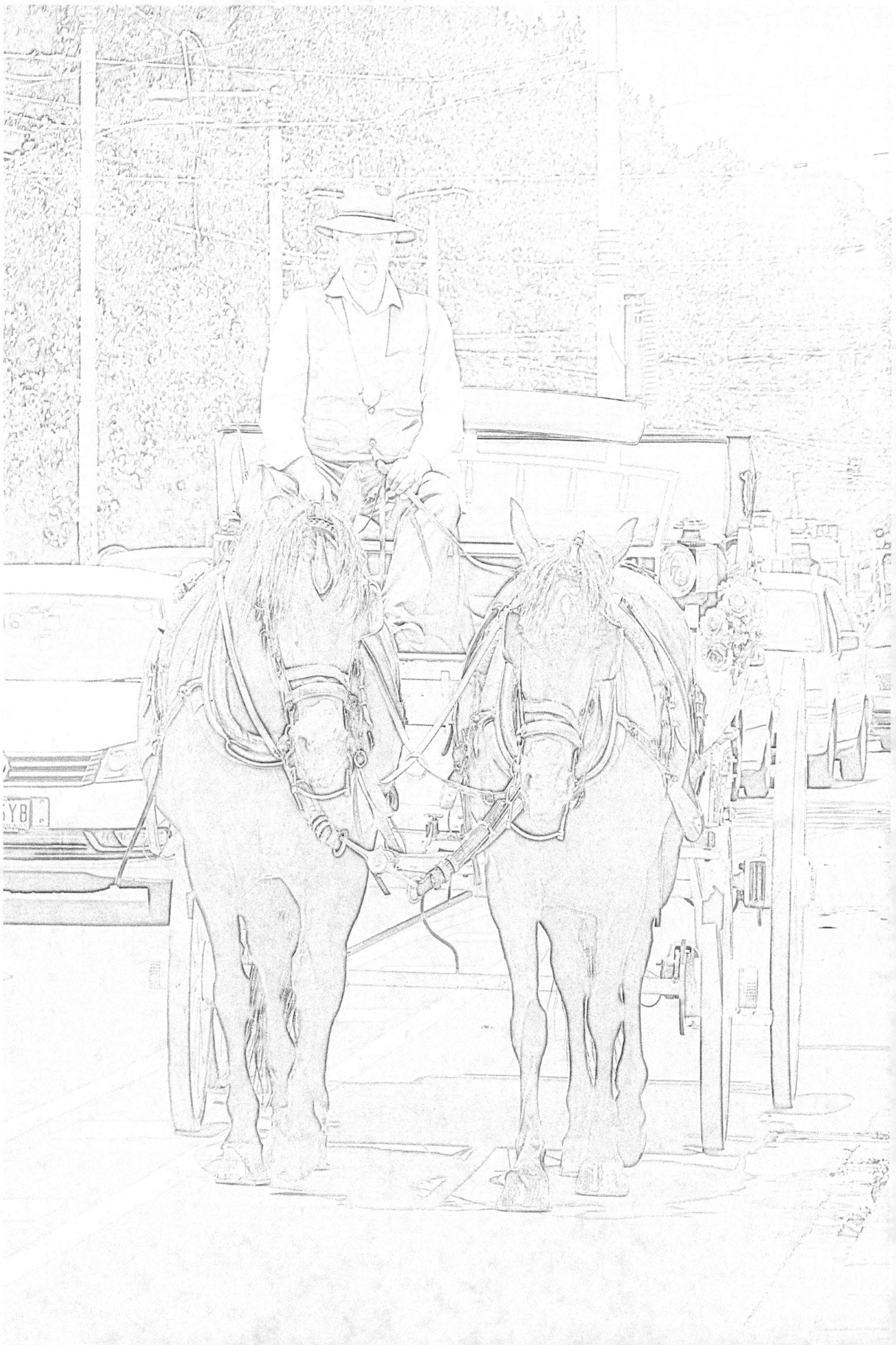
5YB

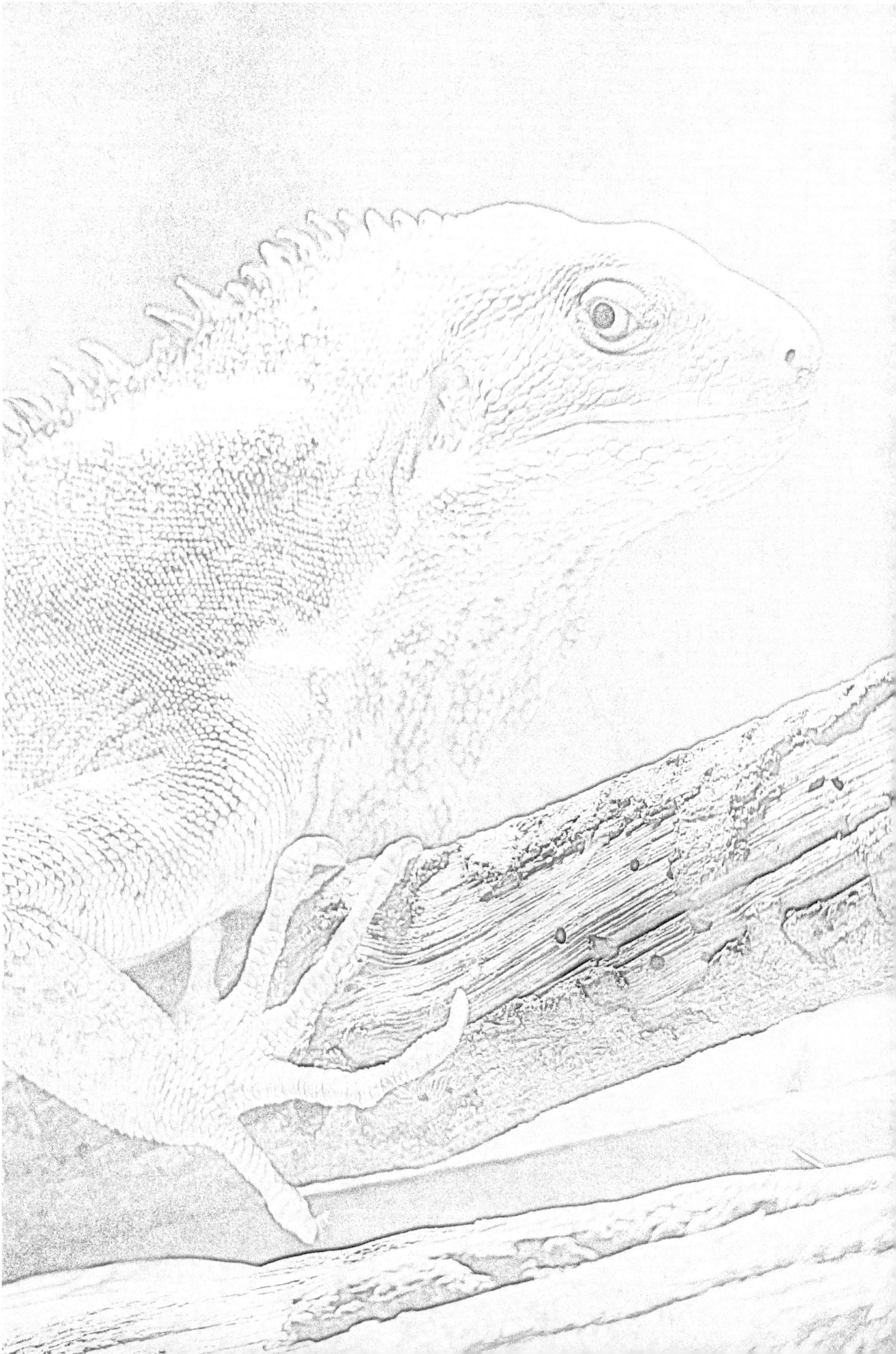

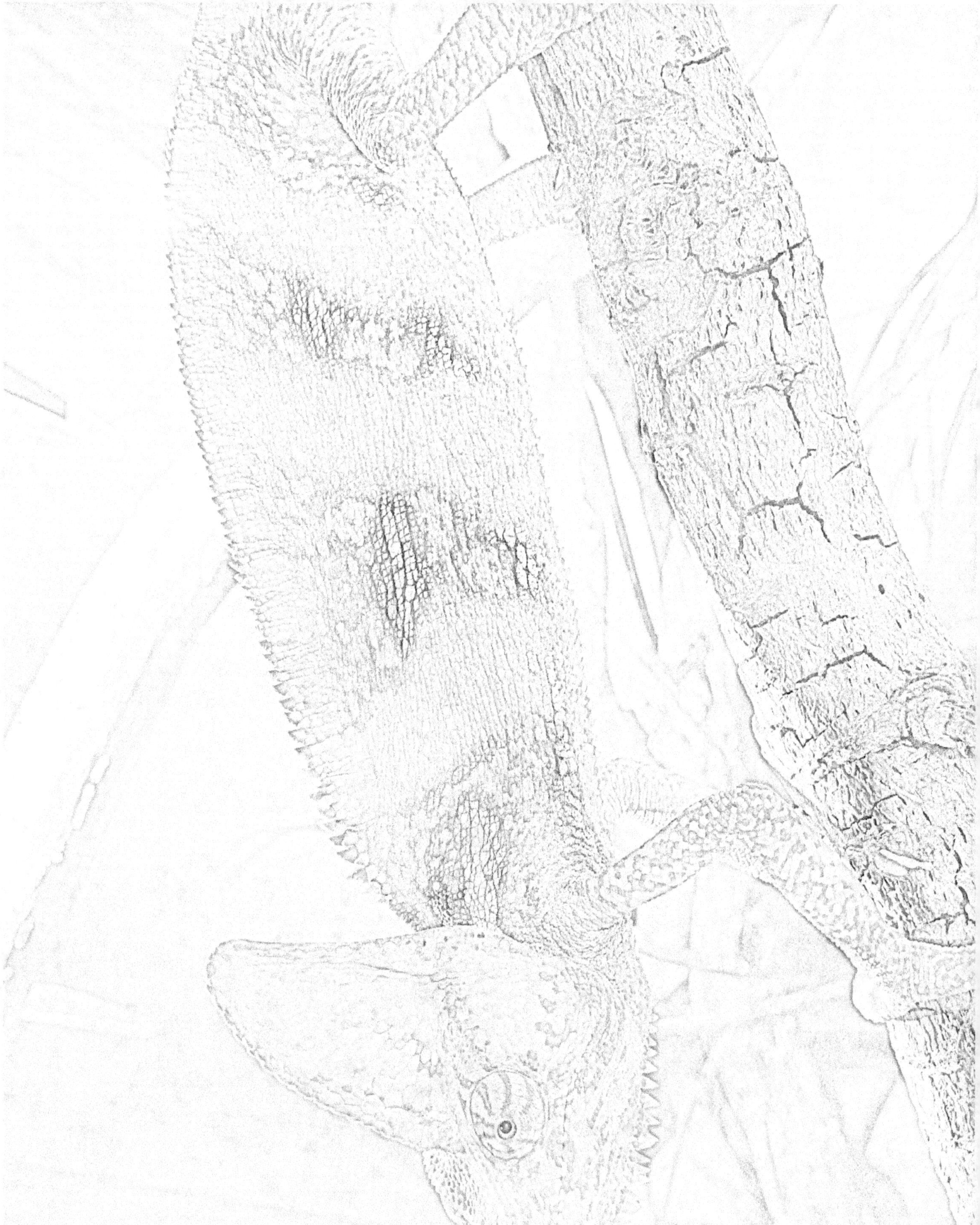

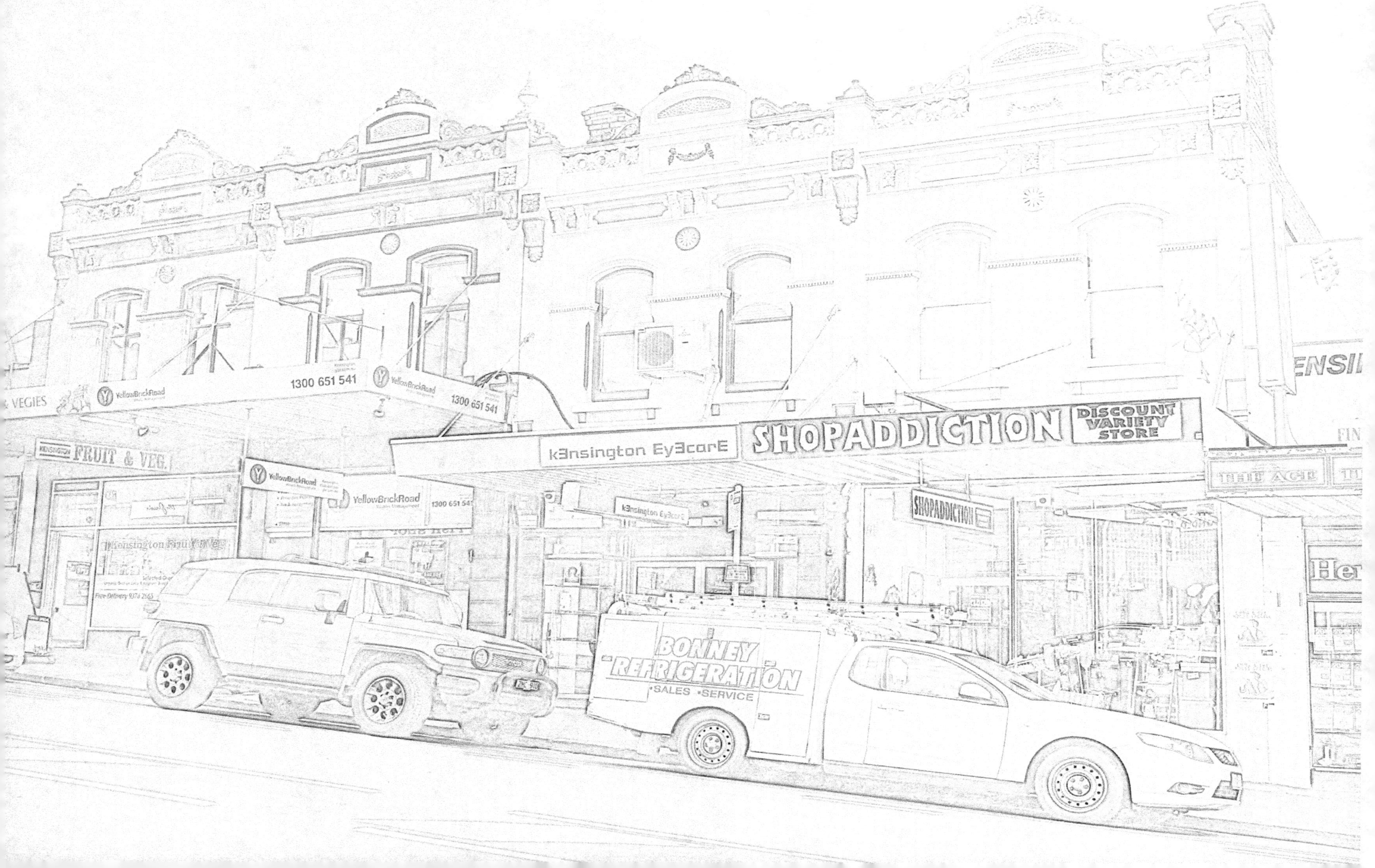
SHOPADDICTION
DISCOUNT VARIETY STORE
k3nsington Ey3carE
KENSINGTON FRUIT & VEG.
VEGIES
YellowBrickRoad
1300 651 541
BONNEY REFRIGERATION
•SALES •SERVICE
THE AGE

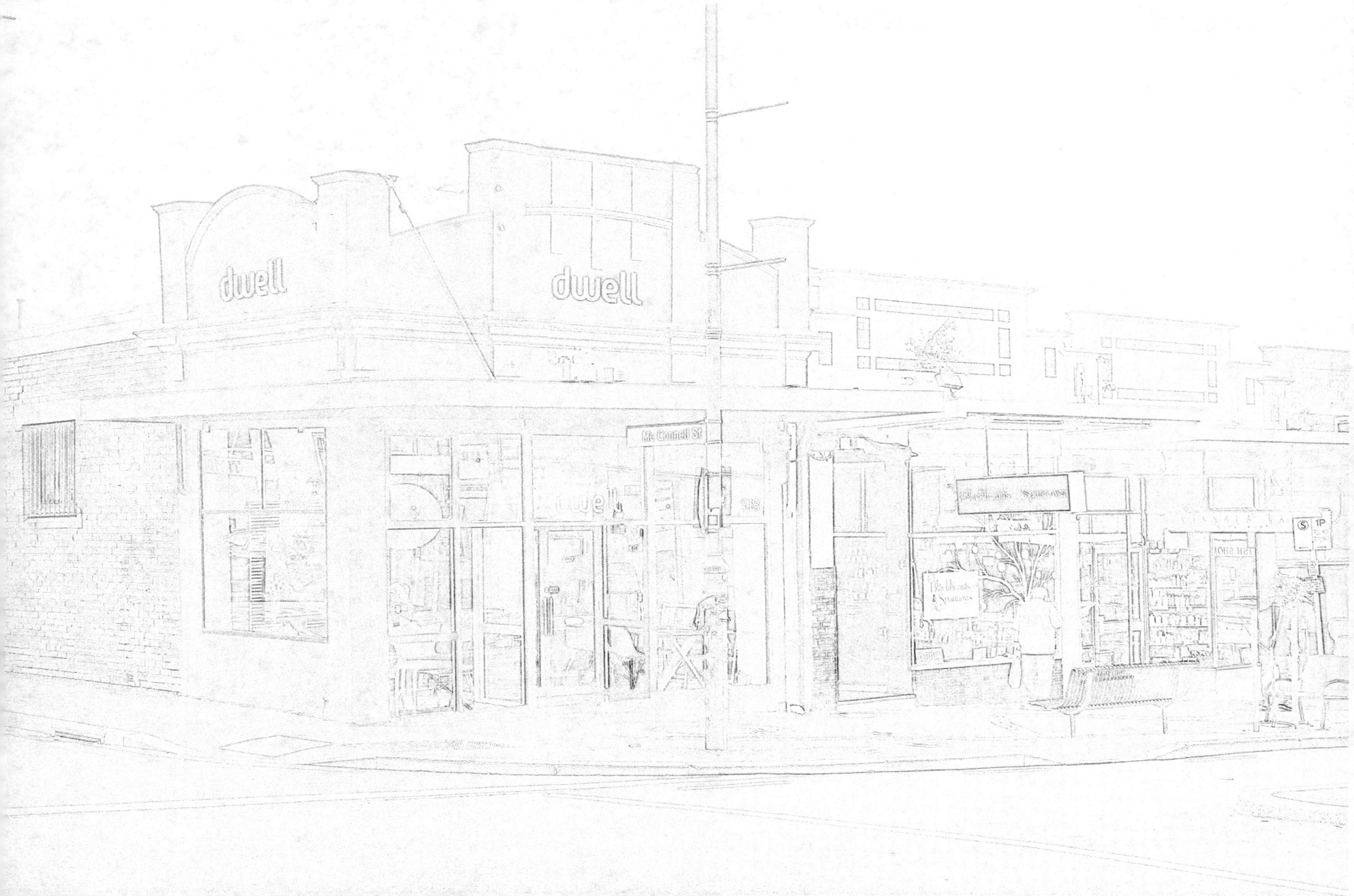
dwell
dwell
Mc Connell St
dwell
1P

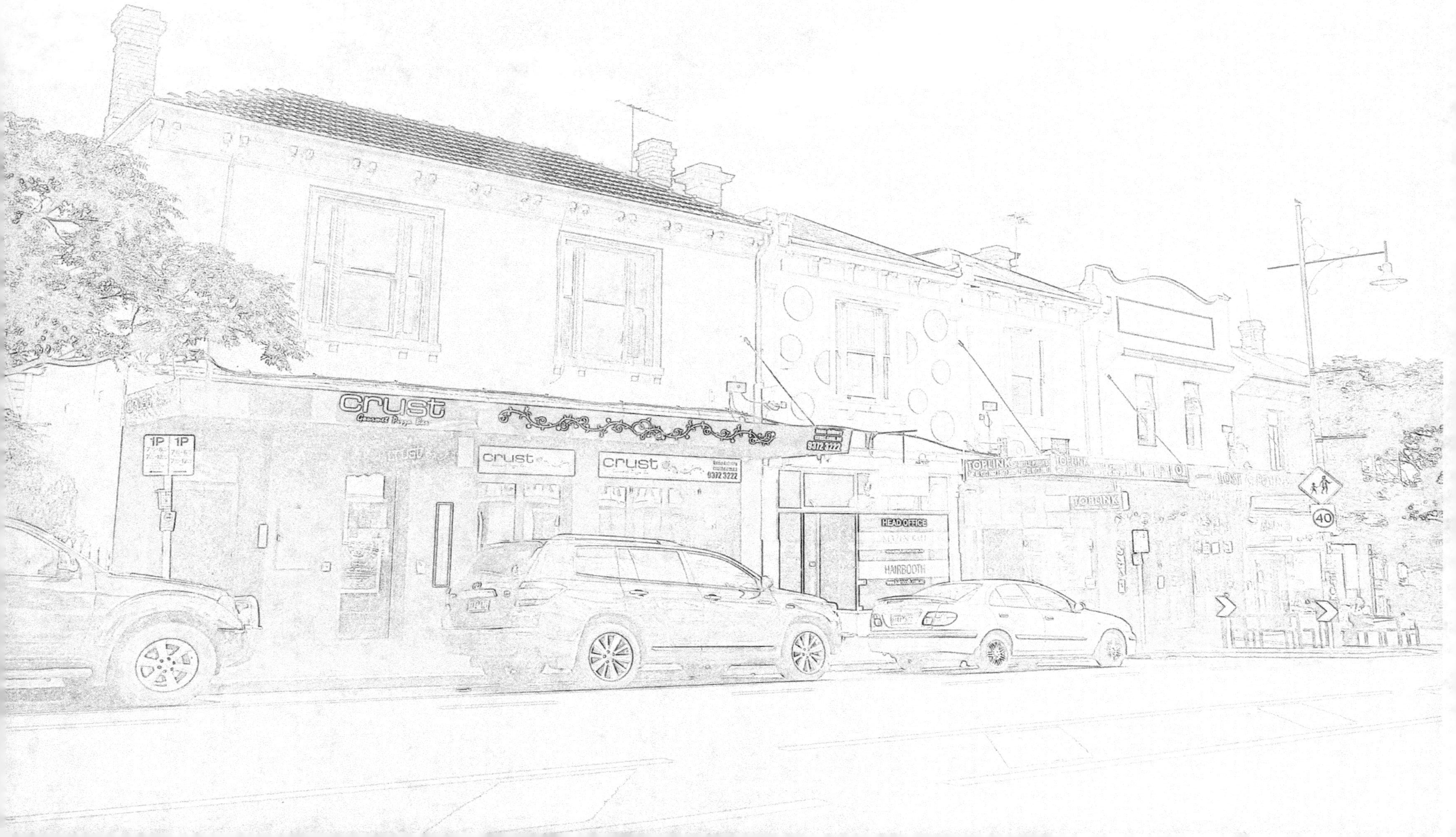
crust
crust
crust
9372 3222
1P
1P
HEAD OFFICE
HAIRBOOTH
TOPLINK
TOPLINK
40

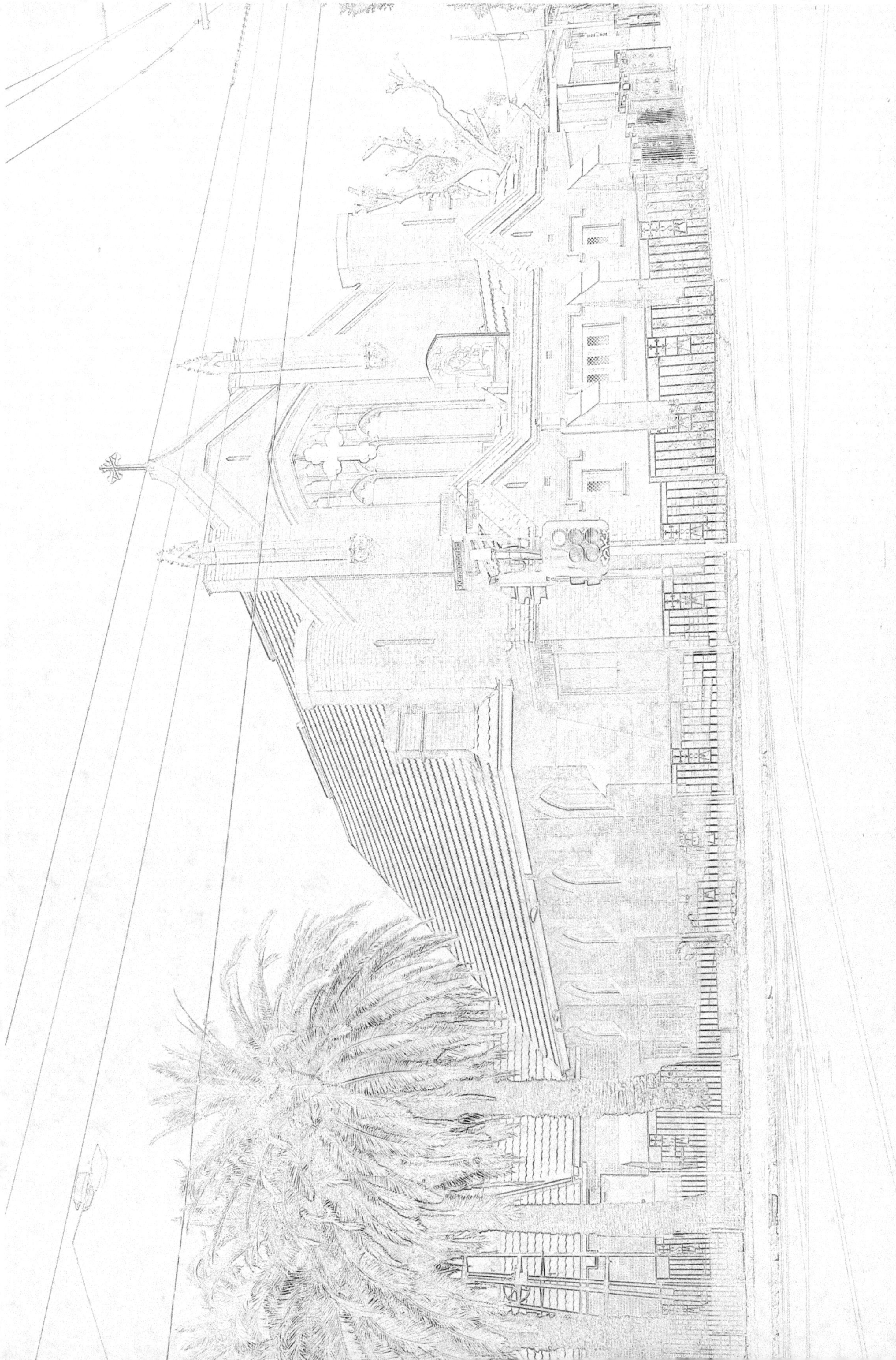

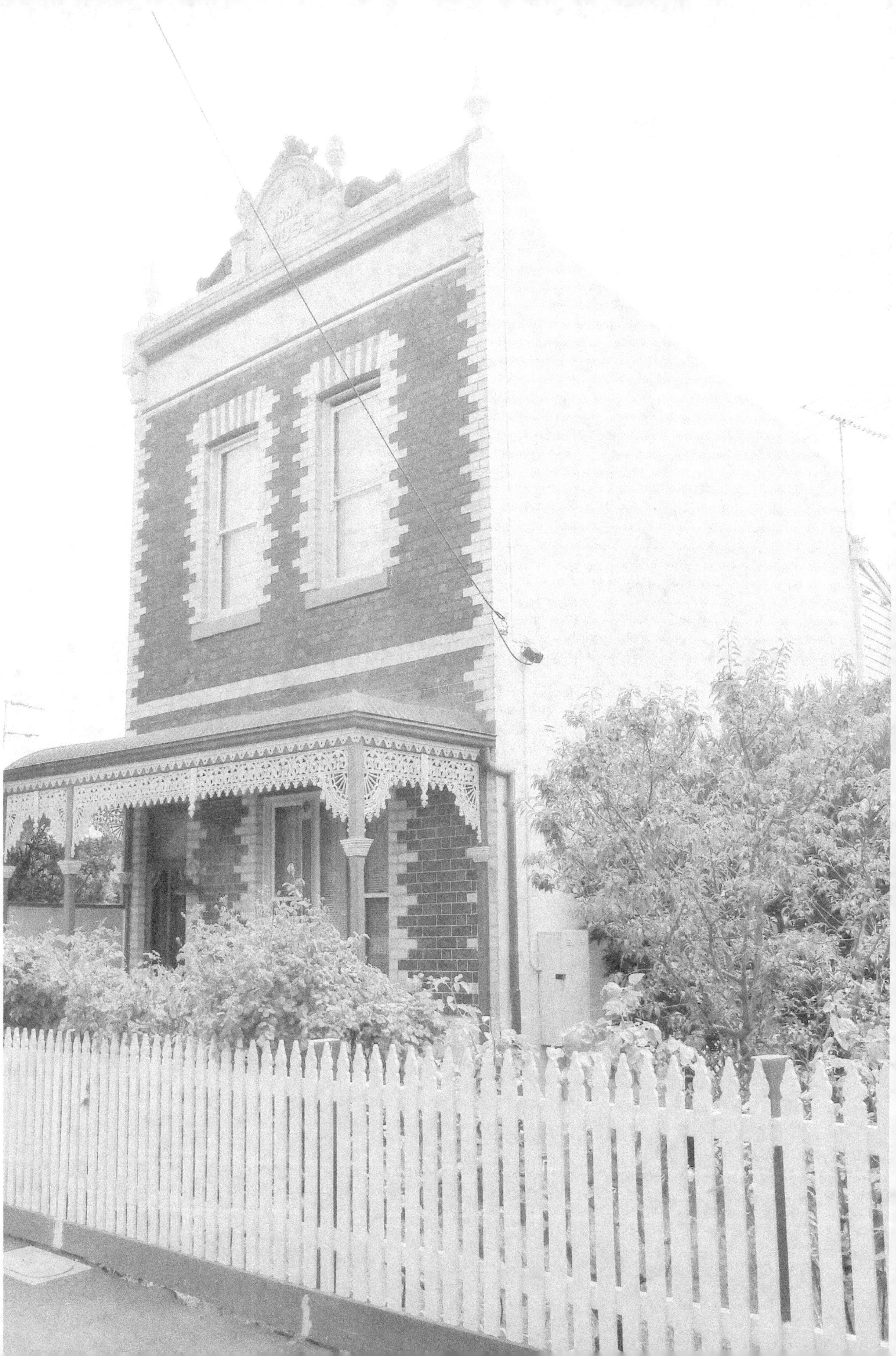

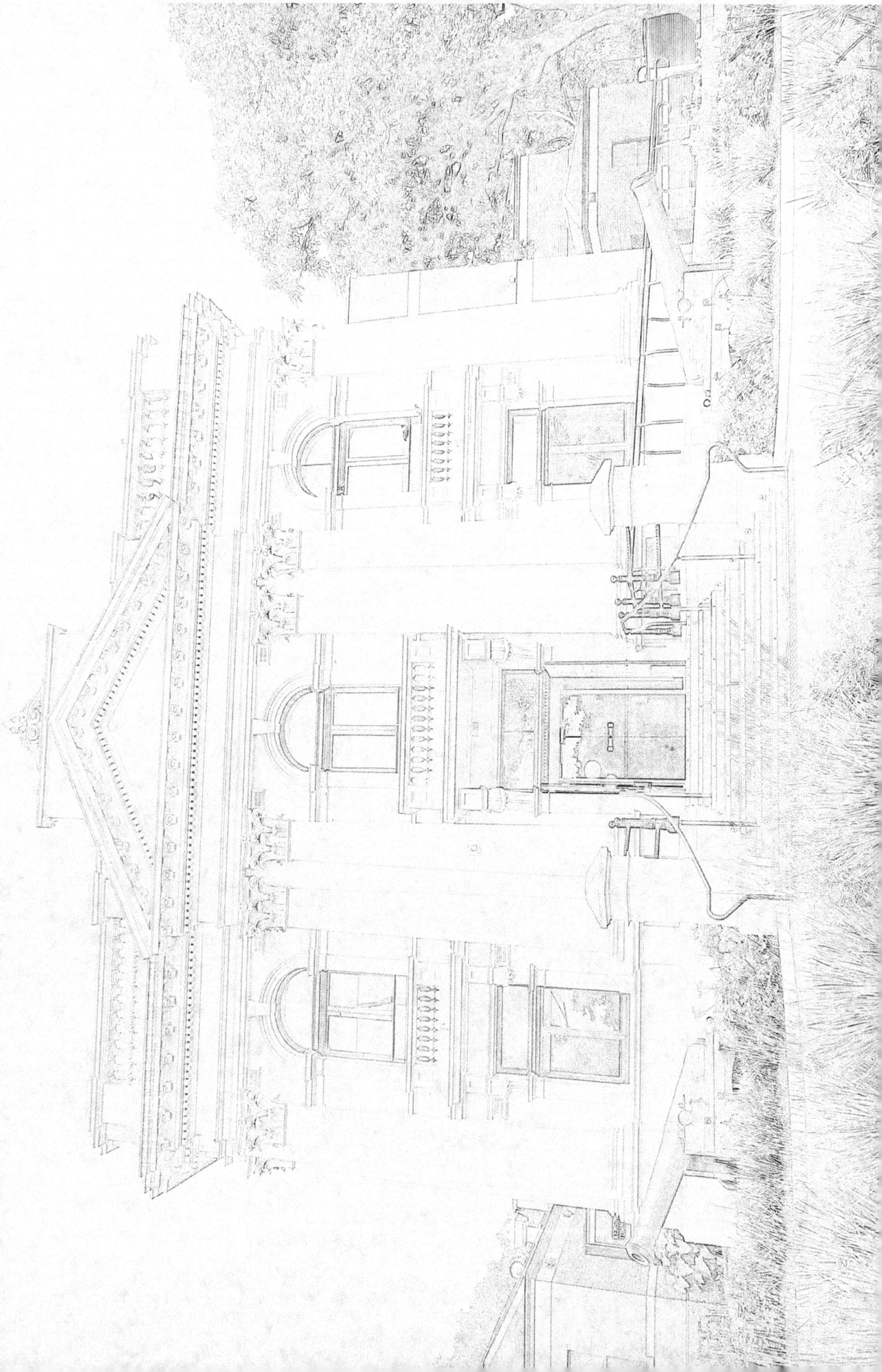

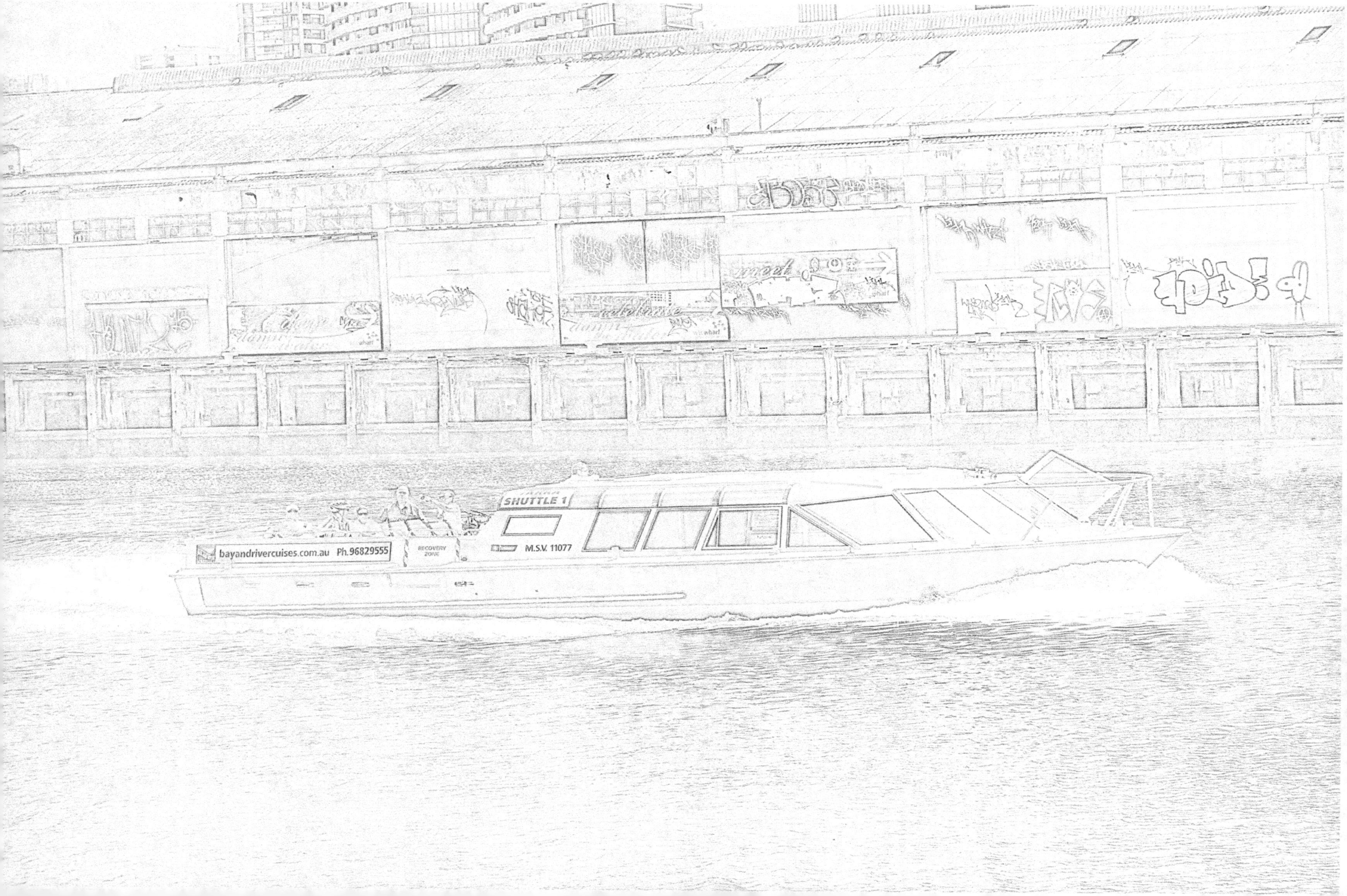
SHUTTLE 1
M.S.V. 11077
bayandrivercuises.com.au Ph.96829555
RECOVERY ZONE

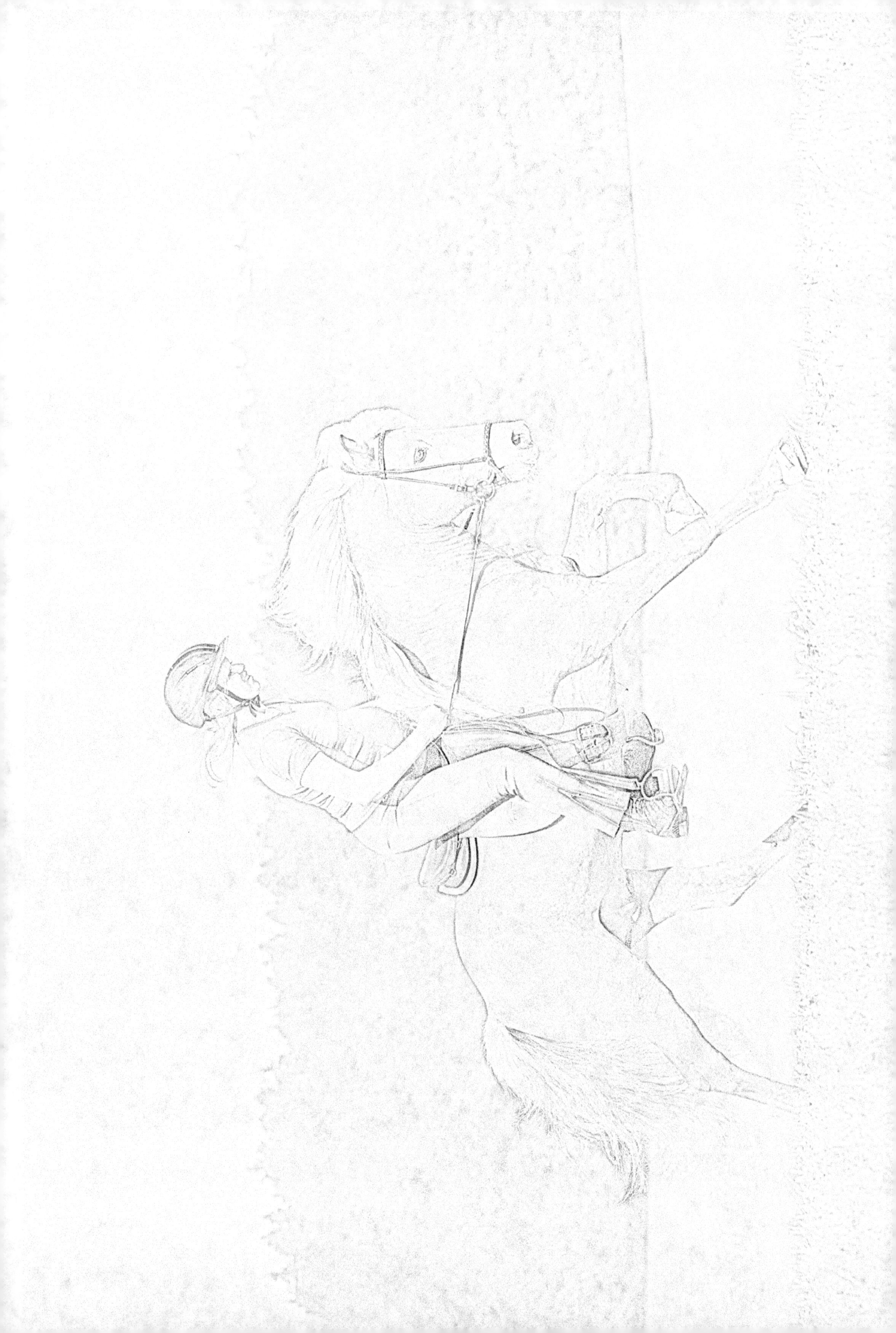

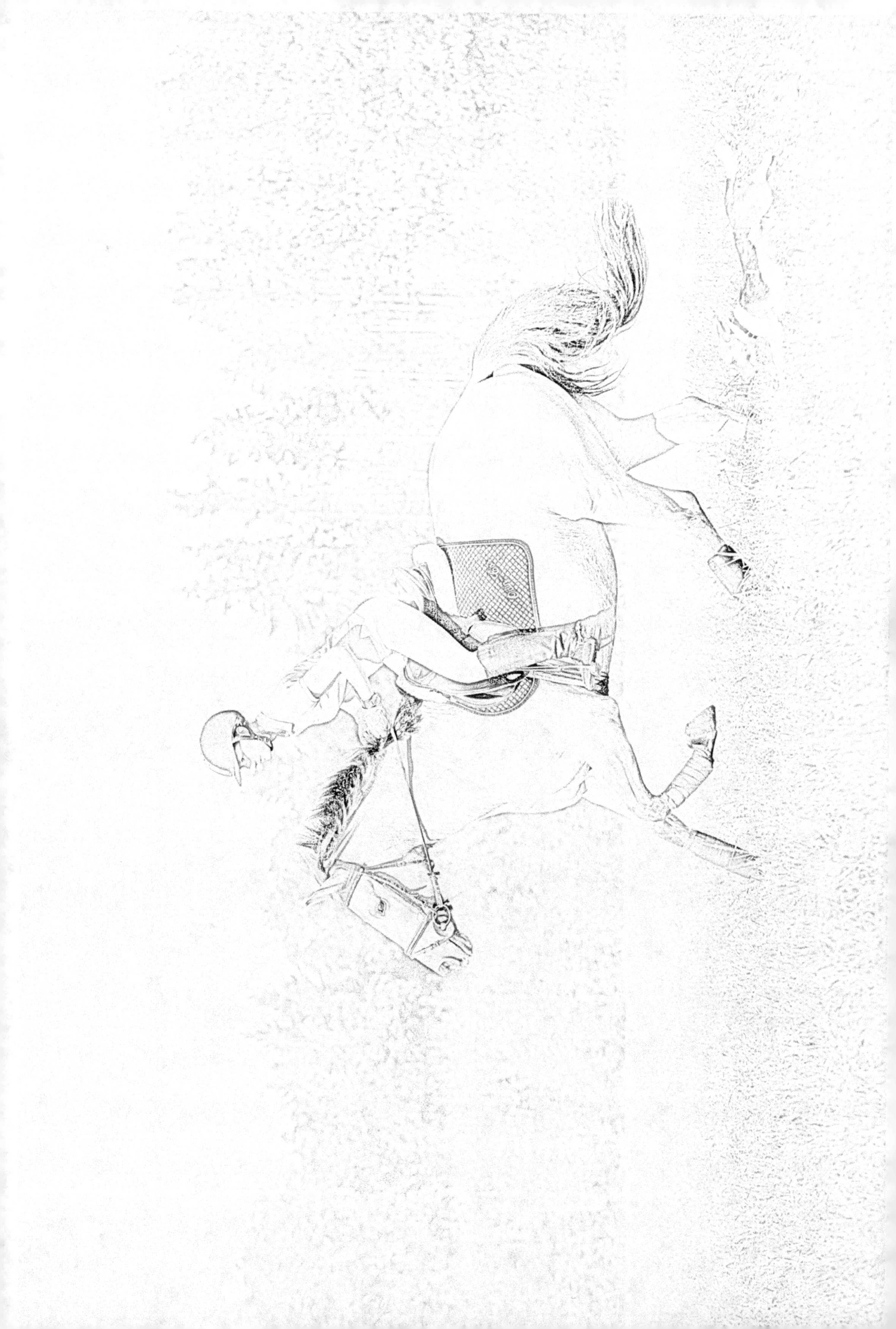

www.ingramcontent.com/pod-product-compliance
Lightning Source LLC
Chambersburg PA
CBHW081051180526
45170CB00005B/1763